THE DEBATE OVER THERMONUCLEAR STRATEGY

Problems in American Civilization

UNDER THE EDITORIAL DIRECTION OF *George Rogers Taylor*

THE DEBATE OVER
THERMONUCLEAR STRATEGY

EDITED WITH AN INTRODUCTION BY

Arthur I. Waskow

INSTITUTE FOR POLICY STUDIES

Problems in American Civilization

D. C. HEATH AND COMPANY: Boston

ENGLEWOOD · CHICAGO · DALLAS · SAN FRANCISCO · ATLANTA · LONDON · TORONTO

65-6618 ✓

INTRODUCTION

By placing Sputnik in orbit, the Soviet Union demonstrated in 1957 that intercontinental missiles carrying thermonuclear warheads could be projected from one point of the earth to another in a matter of minutes. An intercontinental rocket with an H-bomb on its tip made it possible for a few men quickly and effectively to destroy millions of people in far distant lands. This new situation challenged all previous assumptions about national defense. Says Kenneth Boulding:

It is the increase in the range of the projectile that has come with the airplane and the missile . . . that has caused the dramatic breakdown in the system of national defense as we see it today. . . . For national defense as a system to possess any kind of equilibrium and for nations to be unconditionally viable under a system of national defense, each nation must be able to preserve an area of peace within its critical boundaries even if it has to maintain this area of peace by fighting wars outside it. Each nation must also be stronger than its potential enemies, or even any reasonably probable combination of them, within its critical boundaries, and it must be weaker than its enemies within their critical boundaries. If, because of the increasing range of projectiles, the critical boundary must now extend far beyond the legal boundary in order to give any kind of security, the chances of a viable system of national defense fall to zero. Violence can now jump any boundary, and the ancient concept of defense symbolized by the wall, whether the walled city, the Great Wall of China, the Maginot line, or even DEW line, has crumbled in ruins.[1]

So, as C. Vann Woodward points out in the first item in this volume of readings, the "era of free security" has ended. Now military men, politicians, and scholars must work out new strategies for national defense. Three basically different approaches have emerged in this post-Sputnik debate.

The first of these developed as a reaction to the assumptions dominating American nuclear strategy before Sputnik. The old strategy had been governed by two major assumptions: that any thermonuclear war was sure to be utterly unmanageable and might well turn out to be infinitely frightful; but that such a war could almost certainly be deterred because of the overwhelming superiority of the United States in ability to deliver a thermonuclear attack. Thus thermonuclear strategy rested on a "balance of terror," and its stability depended on the superior weight found on the American side of the scales. If American H-bombs were ever to be used, it would be an all-or-nothing proposition.

What threat might provoke such a massive American H-bomb attack was not always clear during the Eisenhower years. John Foster Dulles, Secretary of State under President Eisenhower, an-

[1] Kenneth Boulding, *Conflict and Defense* (New York): Harper and Row, 1962), pp. 267–268. Reprinted with the permission of the publisher.

nounced early in 1954 a strategy of "massive retaliation" whereby nuclear weapons might be used even in retaliation against a non-nuclear attack. In fact, however, the American superiority in nuclear weapons was usually treated during the Eisenhower years as if it were intended solely as a deterrent to Soviet nuclear attack, rather than as an ordinary weapon.

In the wake of Sputnik many feared the balance of terror might be reversed, because American superiority seemed endangered. Albert Wohlstetter, in an influential article reprinted below, warned that the balance had become very "delicate" and suggested that the United States build more weapons and make them less vulnerable to Soviet attack.

In this way, Wohlstetter set the tone of a discussion that began to focus on how to manage thermonuclear war so that if American nuclear superiority were preserved, the weapons could be used in some controlled way rather than in a massive, utterly unmanageable "spasm" war. This approach made up the first of three new strategies. Its proponents emphasized the belief that so long as real conflicts existed between great world powers, it was likely that the balance of terror would someday come unbalanced, that deterrence would fail, and that thermonuclear war would erupt. For that reason, these strategists argued, ways must be found of preparing to use thermonuclear weapons in such controlled, rational ways that their use need not bring about the total destruction of the warring societies. The strategists of *controlled thermonuclear war* wanted to prepare measures that would make it possible to keep the war under control. Such measures might include aiming attacks at enemy missile bases instead of enemy cities; building elaborate systems for gathering and re-laying information on the progress of the war, relaying commands from headquarters to the attack forces; and protecting civilian populations through massive programs of anti-missile missiles and civil defense. Some of the implications and expected uses of this strategy are set forth in the articles by Herman Kahn and Secretary of Defense Robert McNamara. McNamara particularly stresses the hope that preparing for controlled thermonuclear war will enable the United States to cope with a large number of possible military situations and to choose among a great number of "options" if war should come.

But as the strategy of controlled thermonuclear war became more and more elaborate, objections became more frequent and coherent. Sir Solly Zuckerman warned against depending on fighting any war, least of all a thermonuclear war, in the extremely controlled fashion that would be necessary if populations were to be spared and only military forces attacked. He also objected to the whole intellectual process by which many of the strategists were making their calculations. As an alternative to the strategy of "controlled thermonuclear war" there was a revival—with some differences—of the notion that nuclear weapons were chiefly to be viewed as a deterrent. The major difference was that many of the weaknesses which the controlled-strategy analysts had exposed in the old balance of terror were acknowledged, and efforts made to correct them. The paper by Leo Szilard sets forth the more sophisticated strategy of a *minimal deterrent* based on a small number of practically invulnerable nuclear missiles. Szilard thus argues that the dangers of a "spasm war," which Wohlstetter criticized, might be avoided without engaging in an infinite search for more and better weapons with which to fight controlled thermonuclear wars. Perhaps the most important new departure of the minimal-deterrent strategists was the argument that deterrence need not necessarily rest on a great American superiority, but could easily—indeed more safely—depend on approximate nuclear parity between the two giants.

Simultaneously there began to develop a third school of strategy, the most unorthodox in that it called for world-wide *disarmament* as the most effective military means of protecting national security. This approach was new in that it did not regard disarmament chiefly as an ultimate ethical imperative. Nor was disarmament seen as a way of attaining a wholly new world of harmony and law. It was now looked upon as the best way of safeguarding national interests: in short, as a strategy rather than a utopia. The strategists of disarmament accepted the belief of the "controlled war" strategists that as long as thermonuclear weapons existed, thermonuclear war would be likely; and they also accepted the belief of "minimal deterrent" strategists that if thermonuclear war occurred at all it would be extremely unlikely to stay controlled. For these reasons, the disarmament strategists thought it necessary to eliminate the weapons.

The most weighty support for this strategy came from President John F. Kennedy in committing the United States to seeking world disarmament, and one of the most important dissents came from Senator Barry M. Goldwater who argued that such strategy would endanger American security. The debate was carried on in the scholarly as well as the political world. Such experts as Charles Osgood, Robert Strausz-Hupé, Thomas Schelling, and Walter Millis explored the conditions under which disarmament might or might not, should or should not be achieved,

and suggested the kinds of world that might result.

The debate among the three schools of strategists frequently ignored the deeper political questions in which military strategy was embedded. Both C. Vann Woodward and Senator J. William Fulbright emphasized that decisions on military strategy were deeply affecting American society and might be changing it in ways not taken into account by the strategists. Fulbright also pointed out that many strategic assumptions—in all three schools of strategy—depended on the continued existence of the Cold War and a bipolar world. Speaking early in 1964, after the nuclear test ban treaty had been concluded and after both China and France had demonstrated their independence of the old alliances, Fulbright suggested that international politics might be changing in such basic ways that a thorough reexamination of strategy was needed.

Thus, eight years after Sputnik some of the terms of the debate over strategy are changing. The political implications of thermonuclear strategy for the future of the Atlantic Alliance and the whole Cold War, of the "Third World" of hungry nations, and indeed of the politics and society of America itself are becoming more important in the debate. But always at the heart of the matter, giving it unprecedented urgency and complexity, are the questions of how to deal with the bomb itself. Will it someday inevitably be used? Can it conceivably be eliminated? Is there any way to keep it permanently under control without disarmament? Might there even be ways to control the use of the bomb if it ever came to that?

However the debate develops, the decision will almost certainly come down to choices among some variants of the three basic strategies: to keep thermonuclear weapons and try to prepare to use them in controlled ways; to keep them solely as deterrents, in the knowledge that if any nation used them, total destruction would be the most likely result; or to try to get rid of them and build a world free of the threat of war. In each policy are threatened dangers, in each possible attractions. The readings focus attention on these questions of strategy and of survival.

[NOTE: Footnotes have generally been omitted from the selections that follow, except where needed to explain the text.]

CONTENTS

C. Vann Woodward:

THE AGE OF REINTERPRETATION

> *C. Vann Woodward, Sterling Professor of History at Yale University, is widely known for his studies in the history of the American South. His article, reproduced in large part below, alerts his fellow historians and Americans generally, to the problems raised by the creation of thermonuclear weapons. He calls for a bold reinterpretation of American history—a recognition of the profound effect on our earlier development of freedom from the threat of foreign attack; an awareness of the urgent need to rethink America's role in the modern world of deadly missiles.*

THROUGHOUT most of its history the United States has enjoyed a remarkable degree of military security, physical security from hostile attack and invasion. This security was not only remarkably effective, but it was relatively free. Free security was based on nature's gift of three vast bodies of water interposed between this country and any other power that might constitute a serious menace to its safety. There was not only the Atlantic to the east and the Pacific to to the west, but a third body of water, considered so impenetrable as to make us virtually unaware of its importance, the Arctic Ocean and its great ice cap to the north. The security thus provided was free in the sense that it was enjoyed as a bounty of nature in place of the elaborate and costly chains of fortifications and even more expensive armies and navies that took a heavy toll of the treasuries of less fortunate countries and placed severe tax burdens upon the backs of their people. The costly navy that policed and defended the Atlantic was manned and paid for by British subjects for more than a century, while Americans enjoyed the added security afforded without added cost to themselves. In 1861 the United States was maintaining the second largest merchant marine in the world without benefit of a battle fleet. At that time there were only 7,600 men in the United States Navy as compared with more than ten times that number in the British Navy.[1]

Between the second war with England and the Second World War, the United States was blessed with a security so complete and so free that it was able

[1] During Andrew Jackson's administration Alexis de Tocqueville described the situation in the following terms: "The President of the United States is the commander-in-chief of the army, but of an army composed of only six thousand men; he commands the fleet, but the fleet reckons but few sails; he conducts the foreign relations of the Union, but the United States are a nation without neighbors. Separated from the rest of the world by the ocean, and too weak as yet to aim at the dominion of the seas, they have no enemies, and their interests rarely come into contact with those of any other nation of the globe." *Democracy in America,* tr. Henry Reeve (2 vols., New York, 1904), I, 120.

From C. Vann Woodward, "The Age of Reinterpretation," *The American Historical Review,* LXVI (October 1960), pp. 2–13. Reprinted with permission of the author and the publisher.

virtually to do without an army and for the greater part of the period without a navy as well. Between the world war that ended in 1763 and the world wars of the twentieth century the only major military burdens placed upon the people were occasioned not by foreign threats but by domestic quarrels, the first to establish independence for the American colonies and the second to thwart independence for the southern states. After each of these civil wars, as after all the intervening wars, Americans immediately dismantled their military establishment. They followed the same procedure after every succeeding war, down to World War II, and even after that they carried demobilization to dangerous extremes before reversing the policy.

The end of the era of free security has overtaken Americans so suddenly and swiftly that they have not brought themselves to face its practical implications, much less its bearing upon their history. Conventional aircraft and jet propulsion had shrunk the time dimensions of the Atlantic and Pacific from weeks to hours by the mid-fifties. But before military adjustment could be properly made to that revolution, the development of ballistic missiles shrank the two oceans further from hours to minutes. In the same period the hitherto impenetrable Arctic Ocean has not only been navigated by atomic-powered submarines under the ice cap, but has been shrunk in time width to dimensions of minutes and seconds by which we now measure the other oceans. The age of security and the age of free security ended almost simultaneously.

The proposition was advanced before a meeting of the American Historical Association in 1893 that "the first period of American history," a period of four centuries, was brought to an end by the disappearance of free land. Perhaps it is not premature to suggest that another epoch of American history was closed even more suddenly sixty years later by the disappearance of free security. It may be objected that security was never completely free and that the period when it came nearest to being so did not last very long. But one can reasonably ask as much latitude to speak in comparative and relative terms about free security as the theorists of free land enjoyed in their generalizations. Land was of course never completely free either, and the period when it came nearest to being so only dated from the Homestead Act of 1862, less than three decades before the end of the frontier era. In a comparative sense land may nevertheless be said to have been relatively free for a much longer period. In similar terms security may also be said to have been free until quite recently.

Military expenditures of the federal government have, of course, increased greatly and almost continuously since the last decade of the eighteenth century. Until very recently, however, they have not increased so rapidly as the government's nonmilitary expenditures. During the first century of the Republic's history, save in war years, annual military expenditures rarely came to as much as one per cent of the gross national product, returned to that level a few years after the First World War, and remained there until the Great Depression cut production back drastically. In the decade preceding Pearl Harbor, the percentage of federal expenditures devoted to military purposes fell lower than ever before in our history.

Another measure of free security is the small demand that military service has made upon national manpower. Before World War I, apart from actual war periods and their immediate aftermath, it was an extremely rare year in which as many as one per cent of the total male population between the ages of twenty and thirty-nine saw military service. Between Reconstruction and the Spanish-American War there was no year in which as many as one-half of one per cent served in the armed forces. The handful of men who made up the regular army during the nineteenth century were not employed in patrolling frontiers against foreign invasion, but chiefly in coping with a domestic police problem posed by the Indians. Upon the outbreak of the Civil War the United States Army numbered a few more than sixteen thousand men, and 183 of its 198 companies were spread among seventy-nine posts on the Indian frontier. The remaining fifteen companies were available for "defense" of the Canadian and Atlantic frontiers, and the incipient Confederate frontier. The southern constabulary that patrolled the slaves was organized on military lines, but like the regular army it was concerned with a domestic police problem.

The contrast between free security and security costs of the present era scarcely requires emphasis. Military expenditures in 1957 and the years since have amounted to 10 per cent of the gross national product. By way of comparison, military expenditures in the 1880's were never over four-tenths of one per cent. In spite of the vast increase of the gross national product during the last century, military costs have increased far faster and now represent ten to twenty times the percentage of the gross national product they represented in the peace years of the previous century. Not counting payments to veterans, they now account for nearly 70 per cent of the federal budget. The more ad-

vanced and improved military machinery paradoxically requires more instead of less manpower, both military and civilian. The Department of Defense and its branches employ more civilian workers now than did the entire federal government before the Great Depression. Indications are that we are only at the beginning instead of the culmination of expansion in costs and manpower for military purposes and that future expenditures will be larger still.

If historians waited until the disappearance of free land to recognize fully the influence of the frontier-and-free-land experience on American history, perhaps the even more sudden and dramatic disappearance of free security will encourage them to recognize the effect of another distinguishing influence upon our national history. I am not prepared to make any claims about the comparative importance of the two themes, nor do I wish to make or inspire any exaggerations of the influence of free security. But if the influence of free land may be considered significant in the shaping of American character and national history, it is possible that the effect of free security might profitably be studied for contributions to the same ends.

Certain traits that Americans generally regard as desirable, such as democracy, individualism, self-reliance, inventiveness, have been attributed in some measure to the frontier-and-free-land experience. It might be that the sunnier side of the national disposition—the sanguine temperament, the faith in the future, what H. G. Wells once called our "optimistic fatalism"—is also related to a long era of habituation to military security that was effective, reliable, and virtually free. Optimism presupposes a future that is unusually benign and reliably congenial to man's enterprises. Anxieties about security have kept the growth of optimism within bounds among other peoples, but the relative absence of such anxieties in the past has helped, along with other factors, to make optimism a national philosophy in America. The freedom of American youth from the long period of training in military discipline that left its mark upon the youth of nations where it was a routine requirement could hardly have failed to make some contribution to the distinctiveness of national character.

Free security is related at various points to the development of the American economy. So long as an economy of scarcity prevailed in the land the gross national product was not far above the level of subsistence. While the margin was narrow, the demands of an expensive military establishment could have consumed so large a proportion of the surplus above subsistence as to retard seriously the formation of capital. Relative immunity from this drain, on the other hand, enlarged opportunities for the formation of capital and the increase of productivity. Free security was certainly related to light taxes and a permissive government, and they in turn had much to do with the development of the famous American living standard.

Not all the historic influences of free security have been so benign. Tocqueville's classic study of the national character attributes to democracy some familiar patterns of military conduct that might be profitably reexamined in the light of the free security thesis. Tocqueville finds, for example, that "the private soldiers remain most like civilians" in a democracy, that they chafe under discipline with "a restless and turbulent spirit," and that they are "ever ready to go back to their homes" when the fighting is over. With regard to the officer corps he observes that "among a democratic people the choicer minds of the nation are gradually drawn away from the military profession, to seek by other paths distinction, power, and especially wealth." He adds that "among democratic nations in time of peace the military profession is held in little honor and indifferently followed. This want of public favor is a heavy discouragement to the army." Tocqueville may be correct in suggesting democracy as one explanation for these attitudes and patterns of behavior, but no explanation of American attitudes is complete that neglects a national disposition to look upon security as a natural right. What a people half consciously comes to regard as a free gift of nature they are with difficulty persuaded to purchase at high cost in treasure, inconvenience, and harsh discipline. To reward with high honors, prestige, and secure status the professional military men who insist upon these sacrifices in time of peace comes too hard to such people.

The heritage of free and easy security can also be detected behind the disposition to put living standard, private indulgence, and wasteful luxury ahead of vital security requirements. The same heritage can almost certainly be discerned at work in the tendency to plunge into wars first and prepare for them later. The historic background of security might help to explain, even if it cannot excuse, the irresponsibility of political leaders who make foreign commitments, coin bellicose slogans, and indulge in wild threats and promises without first providing the military means to back them up.

There are other aspects of American history besides demagogic diplomacy and military shortcomings that are not to be fully understood without reference to the history of free security. Among these surely is the American Civil War. The United States is the only major country since Cromwellian England that could afford the doubtful luxury of a full-scale civil war of four years without incurring the evils of foreign intervention and occupation. Had such evils been as much a foregone conclusion as they have been among other nations, it is doubtful that Americans would have proved as willing as they were to fall upon each other's throats.

It is doubtful, also, that Americans could have developed and indulged with the freedom they have their peculiar national attitudes toward power, had it not been for their special immunity from the more urgent and dire demands for the employment of power to assure national security and survival. Having this relative immunity, they were able to devise and experiment with elaborate devices to diffuse and atomize power. They divided it among the states and later among business corporations. They used such devices as checks and balances, separation of powers, and division of powers to deadlock power and to thwart positive action for long periods. The experience probably encouraged the tendency to regard power as bad in itself and any means of restraining or denying it as a positive good.

The national myth that America is an innocent nation in a wicked world is associated to some degree in its origins and perpetuation with the experience of free security. That which other nations had of necessity to seek by the sword and defend by incurring the guilt of using it was obtained by the Americans both freely and innocently, at least in their own eyes. They disavowed the engines and instruments of the power they did not need and proclaimed their inno-cence for not using them, while at the same time they passed judgment upon other nations for incurring the guilt inevitably associated with power. "We lived for a century," writes Reinhold Niebuhr, "not only in the illusion but in the reality of innocency in our foreign relations. We lacked the power in the first instance to become involved in the guilt of its use." But we sought to maintain the innocence of our national youth after acquiring power that was incompatible with it. We first concealed from ourselves the reality of power in our economic and technological might, but after it became undeniable, and after military strength was added to it, as Niebuhr says, "we sought for a time to preserve innocency by disavowing the responsibilities of power." The urge to return to a free security age of innocence and the flight from responsibility and from the guilt of wielding power may be traced in elaborate efforts to maintain neutrality, in desperate struggles for isolationism and "America First," as well as in the idealistic plans of religious and secular pacifists.

So long as free land was fertile and arable, and so long as security was not only free but strong and effective, it is no wonder that the world seemed to be America's particular oyster. Now that both free land and free security have disappeared, it is not surprising that the American outlook has altered and the prospect has darkened. The contrast with the past was even sharper in the case of free security than in the instance of free land, for the transition was almost immediate from a security that was both free and effective to an attempt at security that was frightfully costly and seemed terrifyingly ineffective. The spell of the long past of free security might help to account for the faltering and bewildered way in which America faced its new perils and its new responsibilities.

This discussion leads naturally to a second and more extensive field of opportunity for reinterpretation, that of military history. In this field there are no national limitations and few limits of time and period. Military subjects have traditionally occupied a large share of the historian's attention, a disproportionate share in the opinion of some critics. Yet the military historian is now faced with the challenge of relating the whole history of his subject to the vast revolution in military weapons and strategic theory that has occurred in the past fifteen years. Primarily this revolution involves two phases: first, explosives, and second, the means of delivering them upon a target. Both phases were inaugurated toward the end of the Second World War.

The revolution in explosives began when the primitive A-bomb was exploded by American forces over Hiroshima on August 6, 1945.[2] This was the first and, so far, the last such weapon but one ever fired in anger. That event alone marked the lurid dawn of a new age. But the entirely unprecedented pace of change in the weapons revolution has swept us far beyond that primitive dawn and broken the continuity of military tradition and history. Since 1945 we have passed from bombs reckoned in kilotons of TNT to those computed in megatons, the first of which was the hydrogen bomb exploded at Bikini on March 1, 1954, less than a decade after the A-bomb innovation. The twenty kiloton atomic bomb dropped over Nagasaki in 1945 had a thousand times the explosive

power of the largest blockbuster used in World War II, but the twenty megaton thermonuclear bomb represents a thousand-fold increase over the Nagasaki bomb. One bomb half the twenty megaton size is estimated by Henry A. Kissinger to represent *five times the explosive power of all the bombs dropped on Germany during the five years of war and one hundred times those dropped on Japan.* And according to Oskar Morgenstern, "One single bomb can harbor a force greater than all the explosives used by all belligerents in World War II or even greater than all the energy ever used in any form in all previous wars of mankind put together." But this would still not appear to be the ultimate weapon, for it is now said that a country capable of manufacturing the megaton bomb is conceivably capable, should such madness possess it, of producing a "begaton" bomb. Reckoned in billions instead of millions of tons of TNT, it would presumably represent a thousand-fold increase, if such a thing is conceivable, over the megaton weapon.

The revolution in the means of delivering explosives upon targets, like the revolution in explosives, also began during the Second World War. Before the end of that war, the jet-propelled aircraft, the snorkel submarine, the supersonic rocket, and new devices for guiding ships, aircraft, or missiles were all in use. But also as in the case of the revolution in explosives, the revolution in agents of delivery accelerated at an unprecedented pace during the fifteen years following the war. The new jet aircraft became obsolescent in succeeding models before they were in production, sometimes before they came off the drafting boards. The snorkel submarine acquired atomic power and a range of more than fifty thousand miles without

[2] Two rival dates for the opening of the nuclear age are December 2, 1942, when Enrico Fermi established a chain reaction in the Chicago laboratory, and July 16, 1945, when the test bomb was exploded in New Mexico.

refueling. The expansion of rockets in size, range, and speed was even more revolutionary. The German V-2 in use against London during the last year of the war had a range of only about two hundred miles and speed of only about five times that of sound. The intermediary range ballistic missile, capable of carrying a thermonuclear warhead, has a range of around fifteen hundred miles, and the intercontinental missile with similar capabilities has a range in excess of five thousand miles and flies at a rate on the order of twenty times the speed of sound. To appreciate the pace and extent of the revolution in agents of delivery, one should recall that in the long history of firearms, military technology was only able to increase the range of cannon from the few hundred yards of the primitive smoothbore to a maximum of less than thirty miles in the 1940's with the mightiest rifled guns. Then in less than fifteen years ranges became literally astronomical.

In all these measurements and samples of change in military technology it should be kept in mind that the revolution is still in progress and in some areas may well be only in its beginning stages. The line between the intercontinental rockets and some of the space rockets would seem to be a rather arbitrary one. The race for the development of the nuclear-powered plane may produce a craft capable of ranges limited in a practical way only by the endurance of the crew. The technological breakthrough has become a familiar phenomenon of the military revolution, and there is no justification for the assumption that we have seen the last of these developments.

To seek the meaning of this revolution in a comparison with that worked by the advent of firearms is misleading. The progress of the revolution brought on by gunpowder, first used in military operations in the early fourteenth century, was glacial by comparison. Only very gradually did the gun replace the sword, the arrow, the spear, and the battering ram. Flintlocks did not arrive until the seventeenth century, field artillery of significance until the eighteenth century, and it was not until the middle of the last century, more than five hundred years after the first military use of gunfire, that the era of modern firearms really opened. Military doctrine changed even more slowly.

The nuclear revolution is of a different order entirely. If strategic bombing with thermonuclear weapons occurs on an unrestricted scale now entirely possible with existing forces, it is quite likely to render subsequent operation of armies, navies, and air forces not only superfluous but unfeasible. It is not simply that huge concentrations of forces such as were used in major amphibious and land operations in the last world war present a vulnerable target themselves. Of more elemental importance is the fact that such armies, navies, and air forces require thriving industrial economies and huge bases and cannot operate when the cities of their home territories are smoking craters and their ports and bases are piles of radioactive rubble. As for the military effectiveness of survivors in the home territory, according to Bernard Brodie, "the *minimum* destruction and disorganization that one should expect from an unrestricted thermonuclear attack in the future is likely to be too high to permit further meaningful mobilization of war-making capabilities over the short term." Faith in the wartime potential of the American industrial plant would appear to be another casualty of the revolution.

Historic changes in weapons, tactics, and strategy between one war and the next, or even one century or one era and the next in the past, become trivial in importance by comparison with the gulf between the preatomic and the nuclear age of strategic bombing. We are now able to view the past in a new perspective. We can already see that the vast fleets that concentrated off the Normandy beaches and at Leyte Gulf, or the massed armies that grappled in the Battle of the Bulge or across the Russian Steppes, or for that matter the old-fashioned bomber squadrons that droned back and forth across the English Channel year after year dropping what the air force now contemptuously calls "iron bombs" were more closely related to a remote past than to a foreseeable future. They did not, as they seemed at the time, represent the beginning of a new age of warfare. They represented instead the end of an old age, a very old age.

This is not to assume that unrestricted nuclear war is the only type of military operations that are any longer conceivable, nor that wars of limited objectives, limited geographic area, and limited destructiveness are no longer possible. To make such assumptions, indeed, would be either to despair of the future of civilized man or to subscribe to the theory that national differences will thenceforth be settled without resort to force. Even assuming that limited wars may still be fought with "conventional" weapons, tactics, and strategy of the old era, there will still be an important difference setting them apart from prenuclear wars. Where major powers are directly or indirectly involved, at least, limited wars will be fought under an umbrella of nuclear power. The effects of that conditioning environment have yet to be

tested, but it can scarcely be assumed that they will be inconsiderable.

Instead of making military history irrelevant or unimportant, the sudden transition from the old to the new age of warfare should actually enhance the role of the historian. We stand desperately in need of historical reinterpretation. The men who now have responsibility for determining policy, strategy, and tactics in the new age of warfare are inevitably influenced by their experience and training grounded on an earlier age of warfare and an outmoded interpretation of its history. The fact is that many of the precepts, principles, and values derived from past experience in wars can be tragically misleading in the new age. These include some of the so-called "unchanging principles of war" that are imbibed during training and discipline until they become almost "second nature" to the professional military man. Traditions that associate the new type of war with honor, valor, and glory are no longer quite relevant. The sacred doctrine of concentration and mass, applied at the critical point, has lost its traditional meaning.

The age-old assumption of a commander's freedom of choice once war was started can no longer be made. In previous ages, one could start a war and assume that his objectives, methods, or degree of commitment could be altered according to changing prospects of success or failure, or according to whether probable gains outweighed probable losses. Even as late as World War II one could still approach the abyss of barbarism or annihilation, take a look and turn back, settle for an armistice or a compromise, and bide one's time. Once resort is made to unrestricted nuclear war, there is no turning back.

The underpinnings of logic that have

served historically to justify resort to war as the lesser of several evils have shifted or, in their traditional form, quite disappeared. Victory has been deprived of its historical meaning in total war with the new weapons, for the "victor" is likely to sustain such devastation as to lack the means of imposing his will upon the "vanquished." And yet to accomplish this end, according to Karl von Clausewitz, is the rational motive of war. Democratic participation or consent in a war decision is rendered most unmeaningful at the very time popular involvement in the devastation of war has reached an unprecedented maximum.

The history of war and man's attitudes about it should be reexamined in the light of these developments. Attention has already been profitably directed in particular to the question of how and why total war came to appear the "normal" type of conflict between major powers. Such investigation might reveal how military planning became divorced from political planning and war became an end in itself rather than a means of achieving more or less rational political ends. Given the destructive military capabilities presently at the disposal of major powers, it would seem to be more interesting than it has ever been before to learn how and why powers have been willing at some times in history to wage wars with more limited objectives than unconditional surrender, total victory, or complete annihilation of the enemy.

That mankind should have carried the values and precepts of the age of firearms into the thermonuclear age represents a far greater anachronism than the one represented by his carrying the values and precepts of the age of chivalry into the age of firearms. Anachronisms are preeminently the business of historians. The historic service that Cervantes performed with mockery in 1605, when he published the first volume of *Don Quixote*, three centuries after the advent of firearms, cannot with safety be deferred that long after the advent of nuclear weapons. Lacking a Cervantes, historians might with their own methods help to expose what may well be the most perilous anachronism in history.

Albert Wohlstetter:

THE DELICATE BALANCE
OF TERROR

Much of the expert thought that informed and underlay the debate over thermonuclear strategy came from a new profession of "defense intellectuals" working in a new kind of institution, the non-profit research corporation wholly or chiefly involved in contract work for the armed forces. Among these so-called "think tanks," the RAND Corporation in Santa Monica, California, was perhaps the most important; and Albert Wohlstetter, a long-time member of its staff, was one of the most influential of the new defense intellectuals. Here he explains why he fears that the development of missile forces after Sputnik will not automatically keep the balance of terror in balance, and sets the tone within which there evolved the strategic theory of controlled thermonuclear war.

THE first shock administered by the Soviet launching of Sputnik has almost dissipated. The flurry of statements and investigations and improvised responses has died down, leaving a small residue: a slight increase in the schedule of bomber and ballistic missile production, with a resulting small increment in our defense expenditures for the current fiscal year; a considerable enthusiasm for space travel; and some stirrings of interest in the teaching of mathematics and physics in the secondary schools. Western defense policy has almost returned to the level of activity and the emphasis suited to the basic assumptions which were controlling before Sputnik.

One of the most important of these assumptions—that a general thermonuclear war is extremely unlikely—is held in common by most of the critics of our defense policy as well as by its proponents. Because of its crucial role in the Western strategy of defense, I should like to examine the stability of the thermonuclear balance which, it is generally supposed, would make aggression irrational or even insane. The balance, I believe, is in fact precarious, and this fact has critical implications for policy. Deterrence in the 1960's is neither assured nor impossible but will be the product of sustained intelligent effort and hard choices, responsibly made. As a major illustration important both for defense and foreign policy, I shall treat the particularly stringent conditions for deterrence which affect forces based close to the enemy, whether they are U.S. forces or those of our allies, under single or joint control. I shall comment also on the inadequacy as well as the necessity of deterrence, on the problem of accidental outbreak of war, and on disarmament.

From Albert Wohlstetter, "The Delicate Balance of Terror," *Foreign Affairs*, XXXVII (January 1959), pp. 211–34. Copyright by the Council on Foreign Relations, Inc. Reprinted by permission.

II. THE PRESUMED AUTOMATIC BALANCE

I emphasize that requirements for deterrence are stringent. We have heard so much about the atomic stalemate and the receding probability of war which it has produced that this may strike the reader as something of an exaggeration. Is deterrence a necessary consequence of both sides having a nuclear delivery capability, and is all-out war nearly obsolete? Is mutual extinction the only outcome of a general war? This belief, frequently expressed by references to Mr. Oppenheimer's simile of the two scorpions in a bottle, is perhaps the prevalent one. It is held by a very eminent and diverse group of people—in England by Sir Winston Churchill, P. M. S. Blackett, Sir John Slessor, Admiral Buzzard, and many others; in France by such figures as Raymond Aron, General Gallois, and General Gazin; in this country by the titular heads of both parties as well as almost all writers on military and foreign affairs, by both Henry Kissinger and his critic, James E. King, Jr., and by George Kennan as well as Dean Acheson. Mr. Kennan refers to American concern about surprise attack as simply obsessive; and many people have drawn the consequence of the stalemate as has Blackett, who states: "If it is in fact true, as most current opinion holds, that strategic air power has abolished global war, then an urgent problem for the West is to assess how little effort must be put into it to keep global war abolished." If peace were founded firmly on mutual terror, and mutual terror on symmetrical nuclear capabilities, this would be, as Churchill has said, "a melancholy paradox"; none the less a most comforting one.

Deterrence, however, is not automatic. While feasible, it will be much harder to achieve in the 1960s than is generally believed. One of the most disturbing features of current opinion is the underestimation of this difficulty. This is due partly to a misconstruction of the technological race as a problem in matching striking forces, partly to a wishful analysis of the Soviet ability to strike first.

Since Sputnik, the United States has made several moves to assure the world (that is, the enemy, but more especially our allies and ourselves) that we will match or overmatch Soviet technology and, specifically, Soviet offense technology. We have, for example, accelerated the bomber and ballistic missile programs, in particular the intermediate-range ballistic missiles. The problem has been conceived as more or better bombers—or rockets; or Sputniks; or engineers. This has meant confusing deterrence with matching or exceeding the enemy's ability to strike first. Matching weapons, however, misconstrues the nature of the technological race. Not, as is frequently said, because only a few bombs owned by the defender can make aggression fruitless, but because even many might not. One outmoded A-bomb dropped from an obsolete bomber might destroy a great many supersonic jets and ballistic missiles. To deter an attack means being able to strike back in spite of it. It means, in other words, a capability to strike second. In the last year or two there has been a growing awareness of the importance of the distinction between a "strike-first" and a "strike-second" capability, but little, if any, recognition of the implications of this distinction for the balance of terror theory.

Where the published writings have not simply underestimated Soviet capabilities and the advantages of a first strike, they have in general placed artificial constraints on the Soviet use of the capabilities attributed to them. They assume, for example, that the enemy will attack in mass over the Arctic through our Distant Early Warning line, with bombers refueled over Canada—all resulting in plenty of warning. Most hopefully, it is sometimes assumed that such attacks will be preceded by days of visible preparations for moving ground troops. Such assumptions suggest that the Soviet leaders will be rather bumbling or, better, cooperative. However attractive it may be for us to narrow Soviet alternatives to these, they would be low in the order of preference of any reasonable Russians planning war.

III. THE QUANTITATIVE NATURE OF THE PROBLEM AND THE UNCERTAINTIES

In treating Soviet strategies it is important to consider Soviet rather than Western advantage and to consider the strategy of both sides quantitatively. The effectiveness of our own choices will depend on a most complex numerical interaction of Soviet and Western plans. Unfortunately, both the privileged and unprivileged information on these matters is precarious. As a result, competent people have been led into critical error in evaluating the prospects for deterrence. Western journalists have greatly overestimated the difficulties of a Soviet surprise attack with thermonuclear weapons and vastly underestimated the complexity of the Western problem of retaliation.

One intelligent commentator, Richard Rovere, recently expressed the common view: "If the Russians had ten thousand warheads and a missile for each, and we had ten hydrogen bombs and ten obsolete bombers, . . . aggression would still be a folly that would appeal only to an insane adventurer." Mr. Rovere's example is plausible because it assumes implicitly that the defender's hydrogen

bombs will with certainty be visited on the aggressor; then the damage done by the ten bombs seems terrible enough for deterrence, and any more would be simply redundant. This is the basis for the common view. The example raises questions, even assuming the delivery of the ten weapons. For instance, the targets aimed at in retaliation might be sheltered and a quite modest civil defense could hold within tolerable limits the damage done to such city targets by ten delivered bombs. But the essential point is that the weapons would not be very likely to reach their targets. Even if the bombers were dispersed at ten different points, and protected by shelters so blast resistant as to stand up anywhere outside the lip of the bomb crater—even inside the fireball itself—the chances of one of these bombers surviving the huge attack directed at it would be on the order of one in a million. (This calculation takes account of the unreliability and inaccuracy of the missile.) And the damage done by the small minority of these ten planes that might be in the air at the time of the attack, armed and ready to run the gauntlet of an alert air defense system, if not zero, would be very small indeed compared to damage that Russia has suffered in the past. For Mr. Rovere, like many other writers on this subject, numerical superiority is not important at all.

For Joseph Alsop, on the other hand, it is important, but the superiority is on our side. Mr. Alsop recently enunciated as one of the four rules of nuclear war: "The aggressor's problem is astronomically difficult; and the aggressor requires an overwhelming superiority of force." There are, he believes, no fewer than 400 SAC bases in the NATO nations alone and many more elsewhere, all of which would have to be attacked in a very short space of time. The "thousands of coordinated air sorties and/or missile firings," he concludes, are not feasible. Mr. Alsop's argument is numerical and has the virtue of demonstrating that at least the relative numbers are important. But the numbers he uses are very wide of the mark. He overestimates the number of such bases by a factor of more than ten, and in any case, missile firings on the scale of a thousand or more involve costs that are by no means out of proportion, given the strategic budgets of the great powers. Whether or not thousands are needed depends on the yield and the accuracy of the enemy missiles, something about which it would be a great mistake for us to display confidence.

Perhaps the first step in dispelling the nearly universal optimism about the stability of deterrence would be to recognize the difficulties in analyzing the uncertainties and interactions between our own wide range of choices and the moves open to the Soviets. On our side we must consider an enormous variety of strategic weapons which might compose our force, and for each of these several alternative methods of basing and operation. These are the choices that determine whether a weapons system will have any genuine capability in the realistic circumstances of a war. Besides the B-47E and the B-52 bombers which are in the United States strategic force now, alternatives will include the B-52G (a longer-range version of the B-52); the Mach 2 B 58A bomber and a "growth" version of it; the Mach 3 B-70 bomber; a nuclear-powered bomber possibly carrying long-range air-to-surface missiles; the Dynasoar, a manned glide-rocket; the Thor and the Jupiter, liquid-fueled intermediate-range ballistic missiles; the Snark intercontinental cruise missile; the Atlas and the Titan intercontinental ballistic missiles; the submarine-launched Polaris and Atlantis rockets; and Minuteman, one potential solid-fueled successor to the Thor and Titan; possibly unmanned bombardment satellites; and many others which are not yet gleams in anyone's eye and some that are just that.

The difficulty of describing in a brief article the best mixture of weapons for the long-term future beginning in 1960, their base requirements, their potentiality for stabilizing or upsetting the balance among the great powers, and their implications for the alliance, is not just a matter of space or the constraint of security. The difficulty in fact stems from some rather basic insecurities. These matters are wildly uncertain; we are talking about weapons and vehicles that are some time off and, even if the precise performances currently hoped for and claimed by contractors were in the public domain, it would be a good idea to doubt them.

Recently some of my colleagues picked their way through the graveyard of early claims about various missiles and aircraft: their dates of availability, costs and performance. These claims are seldom revisited or talked about: *de mortuis nil nisi bonum*. The errors were large and almost always in one direction. And the less we knew, the more hopeful we were. Accordingly the missiles benefited in particular. For example, the estimated cost of one missile increased by a factor of over 50—from about $35,000 in 1949 to some $2 million in 1957. This uncertainty is critical. Some but not all of the systems listed can be chosen and the problem of choice is essentially quantitative. The complexities of the problem, if they were more widely understood, would discourage the oracular confidence of writers on the subject of deterrence.

Some of the complexities can be suggested by referring to the successive obstacles to be hurdled by any system providing a capability to strike second, that is, to strike back. Such deterrent systems must have (a) a stable, "steady-state" peacetime operation within feasible budgets (besides the logistic and operational costs there are, for example, problems of false alarms and accidents). They must have also the ability (b) to survive enemy attacks, (c) to make and communicate the decision to retaliate, (d) to reach enemy territory with fuel enough to complete their mission, (e) to penetrate enemy active defenses, that is, fighters and surface-to-air missiles, and (f) to destroy the target in spite of any "passive" civil defense in the form of dispersal or protective construction or evacuation of the target itself.

Within limits the enemy is free to use his offensive and defensive forces so as to exploit the weaknesses of each of our systems. He will also be free, within limits, in the 1960s to choose that composition of forces which will make life as difficult as possible for the various systems we might select. It would be quite wrong to assume that we have the same degree of flexibility or that the uncertainties I have described affect a totalitarian aggressor and the party attacked equally. A totalitarian country can preserve secrecy about the capabilities and disposition of his forces very much better than a Western democracy. And the aggressor has, among other enormous advantages of the first strike, the ability to weigh continually our performance at each of the six barriers and to choose that precise time and circumstance for attack which will reduce uncertainty. It is important not to confuse our un-

certainty with his. Strangely enough, some military commentators have not made this distinction and have founded their certainty of deterrence on the fact simply that there are uncertainties.

Unwarranted optimism is displayed not only in the writings of journalists but in the more analytic writings of professionals. The recent writings of General Gallois parallel rather closely Mr. Alsop's faulty numerical proof that surprise attack is astronomically difficult—except that Gallois' "simple arithmetic" to borrow his own phrase, turns essentially on some assumptions which are at once inexplicit and extremely optimistic with respect to the blast resistance of dispersed missile sites subjected to attack from relatively close range. Mr. Blackett's recent book *Atomic Weapons and East-West Relations*," illustrates the hazards confronting a most able analyst in dealing with the peicemeal information available to the general public. Mr. Blackett, a Nobel prize-winning physicist with wartime experience in military operations research, lucidly summarized the public information available when he was writing in 1956 on weapons for all-out war. But much of his analysis was based on the assumption that H-bombs could not be made small enough to be carried in an intercontinental missile. It is now widely known that intercontinental ballistic missiles will have hydrogen warheads, and this fact, a secret at the time, invalidates Mr. Blackett's calculations and, I might say, much of his optimism on the stability of the balance of terror. In sum, one of the serious obstacles to any widespread rational judgment on these matters of high policy is that critical elements of the problem *have* to be protected by secrecy. However, some of the principal conclusions about deterrence in the early 1960s can be fairly firmly based, and based on public information.

IV. THE DELICACY OF THE BALANCE OF TERROR

The most important conclusion is that we must expect a vast increase in the weight of attack which the Soviets can deliver with little warning, and the growth of a significant Russian capability for an essentially warningless attack. As a result, strategic deterrence, while feasible, will be extremely difficult to achieve, and at critical junctures in the 1960s, we may not have the power to deter attack. Whether we have it or not will depend on some difficult strategic choices as to the future composition of the deterrent forces as well as hard choices on its basing, operations and defense.

Manned bombers will continue to make up the predominant part of our striking force in the early 1960s. None of the popular remedies for their defense will suffice—not, for example, mere increase of alertness (which will be offset by the Soviet's increasing capability for attack without significant warning), nor simple dispersal or sheltering alone or mobility taken by itself, nor a mere piling up of interceptors and defense missiles around SAC bases. Especially extravagant expectations have been placed on the airborne alert—an extreme form of defense by mobility. The impression is rather widespread that one-third of the SAC bombers are in the air and ready for combat at all times. This belief is belied by the public record. According to the Symington Committee Hearings in 1956, our bombers averaged 31 hours of flying per month, which is about 4 percent of the average 732-hour month. An Air Force representative expressed the hope that within a couple of years, with

an increase in the ratio of crews to aircraft, the bombers would reach 45 hours of flight per month—which is 6 percent. This 4 to 6 percent of the force includes bombers partially fueled and without bombs. It is, moreover, only an average, admitting variance down as well as up. Some increase in the number of armed bombers aloft is to be expected. However, for the current generation of bombers, which have been designed for speed and range rather than endurance, a continuous air patrol for one-third of the force would be extremely expensive.

On the other hand, it would be unwise to look for miracles in the new weapons systems, which by the mid-1960s may constitute a considerable portion of the United States force. After the Thor, Atlas and Titan there are a number of promising developments. The solid-fueled rockets, Minuteman and Polaris, promise in particular to be extremely significant components of the deterrent force. Today they are being touted as making the problem of deterrence easy to solve and, in fact, guaranteeing its solution. But none of the new developments in vehicles is likely to do that. For the complex job of deterrence, they all have limitations. The unvarying immoderate claims for each new weapons system should make us wary of the latest "technological breakthroughs." Only a very short time ago the ballistic missile itself was supposed to be intrinsically invulnerable on the ground. It is now more generally understood that its survival is likely to depend on a variety of choices in its defense.

It is hard to talk with confidence about the mid- and late-1960s. A systematic study of an optimal or a good deterrent force which considered all the major factors affecting choice and dealt adequately with the uncertainties would be a formidable task. In lieu of this, I shall mention briefly why none of the many systems available or projected dominates the others in any obvious way. My comments will take the form of a swift run-through of the characteristic advantages and disadvantages of various strategic systems at each of the six successive hurdles mentioned earlier.

The first hurdle to be surmounted is the attainment of a stable, steady-state peacetime operation. Systems which depend for their survival on extreme decentralization of controls, as may be the case with large-scale dispersal and some of the mobile weapons, raise problems of accidents and over a long period of peacetime operation this leads in turn to serious political problems. Systems relying on extensive movement by land, perhaps by truck caravan, are an obvious example; the introduction of these on European roads, as is sometimes suggested, would raise grave questions for the governments of some of our allies. Any extensive increase in the armed air alert will increase the hazard of accident and intensify the concern already expressed among our allies. Some of the proposals for bombardment satellites may involve such hazards of unintended bomb release as to make them out of the question.

The cost to buy and operate various weapons systems must be seriously considered. Some systems buy their ability to negotiate a given hurdle—say, surviving the enemy attack—only at prohibitive cost. Then the number that can be bought out of a given budget will be small and this will affect the relative performance of competing systems at various other hurdles, for example penetrating enemy defenses. Some of the relevant cost comparisons, then, are between competing systems; others concern the extra costs to the enemy of canceling an additional expenditure of our own. For example, some dispersal is essential, though usually it is expensive; if the dispersed bases are within a warning net, dispersal can help to provide warning against some sorts of attack, since it forces the attacker to increase the size of his raid and so makes it more liable to detection as well as somewhat harder to coordinate. But as the sole or principal defense of our offensive force, dispersal has only a brief useful life and can be justified financially only up to a point. For against our costs of construction, maintenance and operation of an additional base must be set the enemy's much lower costs of delivering one extra weapon. And, in general, any feasible degree of dispersal leaves a considerable concentration of value at a single target point. For example, a squadron of heavy bombers costing, with their associated tankers and penetration aids, perhaps $500,000,000 over five years, might be eliminated, if it were otherwise unprotected, by an enemy intercontinental ballistic missile costing perhaps $16,000,-000. After making allowance for the unreliability and inaccuracy of the missile, this means a ratio of some ten for one or better. To achieve safety by *brute* numbers in so unfavorable a competition is not likely to be viable economically or politically. However, a viable peacetime operation is only the first hurdle to be surmounted.

At the second hurdle—surviving the enemy offense—ground alert systems placed deep within a warning net look good against a manned bomber attack, much less good against intercontinental ballistic missiles, and not good at all against ballistic missiles launched from the sea. In the last case, systems such as the Minuteman, which may be sheltered and dispersed as well as alert, would do well. Systems involving launching platforms which are mobile and concealed, such as Polaris submarines, have particular advantage for surviving an enemy offense.

However, there is a third hurdle to be surmounted—namely that of making the decision to retaliate and communicating it. Here, Polaris, the combat air patrol of B-52s, and in fact all of the mobile platforms—under water, on the surface, in the air and above the air—have severe problems. Long distance communication may be jammed and, most important, communication centers may be destroyed.

At the fourth hurdle—ability to reach enemy territory with fuel enough to complete the mission—several of our short-legged systems have operational problems such as coordination with tankers and using bases close to the enemy. For a good many years to come, up to the mid-1960s in fact, this will be a formidable hurdle for the greater part of our deterrent force. . . .

The fifth hurdle is the aggressor's long-range interceptors and close-in missile defenses. To get past these might require large numbers of planes and missiles. (If the high cost of overcoming an earlier obstacle—using extreme dispersal or airborne alert or the like—limits the number of planes or missiles bought, our capability is likely to be penalized disproportionately here.) Or getting through may involve carrying heavy loads of radar decoys, electronic jammers and other aids to defense penetration. For example, vehicles like Minuteman and Polaris, which were made small to facilitate dispersal or mobility, may suffer here because they can carry fewer penetration aids.

At the final hurdle—destroying the target in spite of the passive defenses that may protect it—low-payload and low-accuracy systems, such as Minuteman and Polaris, may be frustrated by blast-resistant shelters. For example, five half-megaton weapons with an average inaccuracy of two miles might be expected to destroy half the population of a city of 900,000, spread over 40 square miles, provided the inhabitants are without shelters. But if they are provided with shelters capable of resisting over-pressures of 100 pounds per square inch, approximately 60 such weapons would be required; and deep rock shelters might force the total up to over a thousand.

Prizes for a retaliatory capability are not distributed for getting over one of these jumps. A system must get over all six. I hope these illustrations will suggest that assuring ourselves the power to strike back after a massive thermonuclear surprise attack is by no means as automatic as is widely believed.

In counteracting the general optimism as to the ease and, in fact, the inevitability of deterrence, I should like to avoid creating the extreme opposite impression. Deterrence demands hard, continuing, intelligent work, but it can be achieved. The job of deterring rational attack by guaranteeing great damage to an aggressor is, for example, very much less difficult than erecting a nearly airtight defense of cities in the face of full-scale thermonuclear surprise attack. Protecting manned bombers and missiles is much easier because they may be dispersed, sheltered or kept mobile, and they can respond to warning with greater speed. Mixtures of these and other defenses with complementary strengths can preserve a powerful remainder after attack. Obviously not all our bombers and missiles need to survive in order to fulfill their mission. To preserve the majority of our cities intact in the face of surprise attack is immensely more difficult, if not impossible. (This does not mean that the aggressor has the same problem in preserving his cities from retaliation by a poorly-protected, badly-damaged force. And it does not mean that *we* should not do more to limit the extent of the catastrophe to our cities in case deterrence fails. I believe we should.) Deterrence, however, provided we work at it, is feasible, and, what is more, it is a crucial objective of national policy.

Herman Kahn:

SOME COMMENTS ON CONTROLLED WAR

Herman Kahn is a physicist who has worked at the RAND Corporation and Hudson Institute on problems of military strategy. His book On Thermonuclear War *stimulated the first widespread discussion of the possibility that thermonuclear wars could be kept under control, and helped bring about a spirited debate over the morality of "calculating" with human lives and deaths on a large scale. Here Kahn "games out" some conceivable thermonuclear wars.*

PERHAPS the most decisive factor affecting the damage done in a thermonuclear war, more decisive even than the size, would be the type of attacks made. Roughly, there are at least five different types corresponding to five different objectives: (1) countervalue, in which the attacker seeks to maximize damage to the things the defender prizes most highly, usually people and property; (2) a major effort at both the countervalue targets and the counterforce targets (strategic forces such as SAC bases, missiles, Polaris submarines, military-control centers, etc.); (3) straight counterforce, in which the attacker seeks to maximize damage to the defender's strategic forces in order to minimize the damage done by the defender's retaliatory attacks; (4) counterforce plus "bonus," in which the attacker concentrates upon the defender's strategic forces but compromises his tactics slightly in order to obtain bonus damage to countervalue targets; and (5) counterforce plus "avoidance," in which the attacker seeks to maximize damage to the defender's strategic forces but is willing to sacrifice some military efficiency to avoid countervalue targets, either for moral reasons or because such targets may be more valuable to the attacker as hostages to be threatened.

While only attacks (3), (4), or (5) seem rational, until recently most of the attention of military and civilian analysts has been focused on (1) and (2). Given these

From Herman Kahn, "Some Comments on Controlled War," in *Limited Strategic War*, eds. Klaus Knorr and Thornton Reed (New York, 1962), pp. 35–60. Reprinted by permission of Frederick A. Praeger, Publishers.

five possibilities, the assumption that a completely or almost completely "uncontrolled" war, as typified by attacks (1) and (2), is inevitable would not seem to be certain. Neither is the contrary assumption certain: that just because an uncontrolled war is not rational it will not occur. In terms of the actual feasibility of controlled thermonuclear war, there are a number of issues. To name a few: (1) Can one cross the threshold of the use of nuclear weapons without an orgiastic spasm of destruction following immediately—or eventually? (2) Assuming that the threshold could be crossed or modified without inevitable general war, would it be sensible and feasible to use less than all of one's capabilities—and, if so, what kinds of new thresholds might one establish? (3) If one goes "all out" in the sense of a maximum effort, would it be sensible and practicable to discriminate as to targets, timing, and tactics, either on a first or a second strike? (4) If so, under what conditions is one set of targeting objectives to be preferred to another?

I shall not attempt here to explore all of these questions in a realistic fashion, but will attempt only to indicate some of the areas in which detailed studies might help provide answers.

A SIMPLE MODEL OF A
BALANCE OF TERROR

In trying to analyze some of the less pleasant and unfamiliar aspects of deterrence, it is illuminating to consider some oversimplified models. These hypothetical models are intended only as the simplest of illustrations of areas that it would be fruitful to study in detail in a realistic context. One can define language, formulate concepts, and discuss and emphasize some elementary principles more clearly by starting with such models than by taking complex examples from the real world. One may of course get into trouble if one then blindly applies the lessons learned from such models to more complicated and realistic problems. But it is better to take the risk that such models may be misused than to forgo all attempts to develop a clear understanding of at least some parts of the problem. In particular it is difficult to discuss what role rationality might play in deterrence and war, unless one first has some ideas of what is or is not rational conduct to contrast with the other possibilities.

Let us start with one of the simplest possible models of a firm balance of terror: two industrial nations, each with all of its people concentrated in 100 cities of equal size. Assume that each nation has 1,000 completely reliable and invulnerable missiles with nuclear warheads, and that each missile can totally destroy a city. Each side thus has the ability to destroy the other's society ten times over. In these circumstances there would be a realitively firm balance of terror; if one side were to attack, the other could retaliate and destroy the attacker's society completely.

With each side capable of killing the other ten times over, it would make no objective difference whether one side or the other increased its forces. Neither side could use effectively more than 100 missiles, and no greater capability could be turned into a bargaining advantage. This is a typical example of what is called "stable deterrence." It is stable to both surprise attack and accident, the latter because both sides will have no incentive to be trigger-happy or careless and every incentive to be prudent.

Such a model, of course, differs materially from the real world. Not all people are in cities; the number and sizes of cities are not symmetrical; weapons systems are not completely reliable and invulnerable; at least today neither side has an "overkill" or even a complete kill capability. And even if there were a reliable mutual overkill capability, in the real world the overkill would not be so stark, and those bemused by older ideas would doubtless feel that if one doubles one's forces, one has somehow increased one's effective strength. Therefore, in spite of a mutual overkill capability, they might still feel more or less confident in conducting their bargaining, depending upon the relative excess number of missiles in their arsenals.

But even disregarding for a moment these limitations, our model is not as stable or peaceful as one might think. Though by assumption we have left out the possibility of a meaningful arms race, either technical or numerical, there will still be pressures to conceive of new ways in which weapons might be used—i.e., pressures toward a strategy race. There are at least five ways in which one side or the other could try to hypothecate its strategic nuclear weapons into a bargaining advantage: (1) by manipulating the threat of war; (2) by exploiting "ban-the-bomb" movements; (3) by a nuclear "show of force"; (4) by administering punishment in the form of a limited nuclear attack; and (5) by initiating a "limited general war." Both (4) and (5) have often been called "limited strategic retaliation," "controlled reprisal," or "controlled countervalue attack." . . .

The Nuclear Show of Force

If deterrence were to fail in the sense that one side provoked the other side and in effect challenged it to "put up or shut up," the challenged party might hesitate to attack all out and thus initiate a mutually homicidal exchange.

For example, imagine a crisis in which both sides are determined to stand firm and yet in which the issues are such that it is impossible to leave them unresolved. Somebody, then, has to give way. Side A might initially feel that it should take some violent action to put pressure on B, perhaps even going so far as to destroy one of B's cities. Such a course would involve great risks of escalation, and A might be wise to give B another chance to back down before going through with its act. In order to show that it means business, it might explode a nuclear weapon high over a city, possibly close enough to break windows, thus giving a demonstration of resolve, recklessness, and committal that would indicate to Side B that Side A really meant what it said. Or it might just drop leaflets on several of B's cities via an ICBM, thus informing B's people and decision-makers that an aggressive act would be performed if they did not back down, and symbolically carrying through the aggressive act. The leaflets could carry explicitly the same message that the act would convey symbolically: "I would not be doing this dangerous kind of thing unless I were willing to do even more dangerous things; in the face of this much resolve, do you not wish to reconsider your position?" Or A might consider it more effective to argue its case or appeal to the mutual desire for peace or other universal values and deemphasize the threatening aspects of the symbolic aggression. In this way, A might minimize the provocation and possibility for an emotional response and yet communicate an extremely potent threat. Side B, of course, would have the choice of replying in kind, escalating a bit by itself, replying at a lower level of violence, ignoring the incident, or backing down. We shall call these possible uses of nuclear weapons and their delivery systems a *nuclear show of force.*

Punishment

In the event of an accomplished provocation—say, a massive border raid by conventional forces with extensive damage and loss of life—the aggrieved nation might choose not to respond with an all-out attack. However, a nuclear show of force would be inadequate to avenge a *fait accompli,* or even to establish a precedent that would be effective in deterring repetitions. In such circumstances, an aggrieved nation could conceivably prefer to "make the punishment fit the crime" and use its nuclear weapons to attack or damage a city or two itself, hoping thereby to deter further provocations. While such action would seriously risk escalation, in the emotional reaction to the provocation the risk might be disregarded or seem less dangerous than the precedent of acquiescence.

Limited General War

Let us consider now an extreme and continuing provocation—say, an all-out invasion of A by B, with B limiting himself to the use of conventional or even tactical nuclear weapons. Assume also that A cannot resist B's invasion with his own tactical forces. If the nuclear show of force indicated . . . above did not stop the invasion, it has been suggested that one tactic a desperate or enraged A might employ would be to destroy one of B's cities and threaten to continue destroying a city a day until B backs down. At this point, B would have several choices. He could, of course, back down and sign a peace treaty ending the limited general war. He could threaten to destroy two cities for one, initiating an exchange that would be likely to escalate further. Or he could threaten to

destroy only one city for one and say: "I will continue until you stop this insane city destruction," meanwhile continuing his invasion. The one-city-for-one is not only costly; it carries with it a risk of further escalation, but clearly less risk than the two-for-one reprisal. The backdown is of course least likely to escalate. If B does decide to back down, he might just sue for peace or ask for a cease-fire, or he might not do so until he had destroyed a city of A's and announced: "In the face of your insane behavior, I have decided to compromise, but you did not get a free ride by forcing me to do so. You, too, lost a city, so do not use this as a precedent in the future. If you try it again, the same thing will happen, and even though you win the issue, you will lose a city in doing so. Possibly the next time you will prefer not to attack, but to withdraw, or negotiate a peace."

In some circumstances, A might go ahead and destroy another city in revenge, but in most circumstances it is hard to believe that he would retaliate in turn. Although A might wish to do so to establish a precedent, the precedent is hardly worth the added risk. No matter how justified A might feel, B is unlikely to let A get away with it. B is too likely both to be enraged and to feel that acquiescence would be the end of B's bargaining power, because A will feel that B will have to give way in the future even if B does not actually believe he has to. And, indeed, B's fears may be justified. Letting A get away with extra damage is likely to encourage A to believe in A's potency and B's weakness.

SOME OBJECTIONS

At this point, the reader may be wondering what relevance, if any, these notions have to the real world. In particular, he is likely to raise three objections.

First, how can anyone envisage, even for the sake of argument, decision-makers and people in general acting this coolly and rationally? Secondly, how could A and B ever agree on what are equivalent cities? By population? By wealth? By production? Are these measured in absolute amounts or as a percentage of the whole country? Are historical associations and cultural values counted? And so on. Third, how stable could such a system be? Surely, even if it worked once or twice, it would eventually escalate into all-out war or at least promote reactions that would force a change. In either case, that would end the system.

While all these objections have great force, I believe I have listed them in order of increasing importance. Most people will find it hard to visualize any decision-maker accepting the loss of a city, but one of the reasons they find this difficult is that they compare the situation with a normal peacetime situation. The comparison should be made with the destructive all-out war, and the reader must fully understand that, *at least in our model*, this destruction really is total. Everybody is killed. Nobody is left. In these circumstances I believe one could expect the decision-makers to prefer the controlled city-exchange to the all-out war. After all, the Germans and the Japanese surrendered without fighting to the last man. They could have continued a hopeless resistance, but surrender was preferable even though it was "against their religion."[1] If the only alternatives are between the all-out

mutually homicidal war and the city-exchange, bizarre and destructive as the city-exchange is, it is not as bizarre and destructive as mutual homicide—even if a confusing doctrine seems to make the latter the more conventional response. While there is doubtless much possibility for accident, miscalculation, irrationality, and even madness, in "the moment of truth," when the decision-makers actually face the grim alternatives, it is by no means certain that the escalation would occur. Of course, the reader may argue, it may not be certain that the escalation would occur, but it is not certain that it will not. Therefore, why are you willing to accept this risk? The answer is . . . that this course is not being advocated as an obviously desirable alternative to a possible compromise; it is being advocated mainly as an alternative to the certainty of the mutual homicide. It may or may not be preferable to some degree of accommodation or appeasement, depending on the actual circumstances. And in the real world—as opposed to our model—it may or may not be preferable to an all-out but controlled war. These last two alternatives are compared at the end of this chapter.

The second objection is much stronger. The ambiguity of what can be justified as an "equitable" exchange is indeed crucial: In many circumstances, it may not be a solvable problem. For this reason, the city-for-city exchange may prove either impossible or too extreme. It might be more feasible to take out a target that is economically or militarily important but relatively free of emotional or cultural associations, such as a gaseous diffusion plant, a bridge, a dam, isolated military bases, and the like. It may also be important to take out targets that seem related to the provocation in some causal or utilitarian

---

[1] The German and Japanese examples differ in one important respect from our model. Surrender did not take place until after many years of fighting and destruction of most of the military capability. In the model, it is envisaged that one side may back down without firing many shots and with its military forces largely undestroyed.

way or have some other quality of appositeness or appropriateness about them....

MORE SIMPLE MODELS

Let us now introduce some variations in our simple model in order to see what further light we can shed upon the bizarre possibilities inherent in modern deterrent systems. Let us start by taking away the assumption of invulnerability. Assume that either side can destroy one of the other's missiles by firing two of its own.[2] Superficially this does not change much. If A fired all of its 1,000 missiles at B and thus used up all of its missiles in destroying only 500 of B's, B would "win." B would have the power to retaliate by complete destruction of all of A's cities. But the balance of terror would be less stable because an arms race would now be possible. Whichever side had greater productive capability or will could start manufacturing more missiles and as soon as it had a ratio of more than two to one, it would be in a position to attack. Now reasonably accurate intelligence information becomes important; without it, one or both sides may feel compelled to procure missiles for fear the other side may achieve a greater than two-to-one advantage. Though both sides have an overkill capability (by a factor of ten) in a first strike directed against the other's cities, their second (retaliatory) strike capabili-

ty may be negligible if the attacker gets enough of an advantage.

In the real world, a potential attacker with a more than two-to-one advantage might still be deterred from attacking. There would be enormous uncertainties and imponderables and, if anything went wrong, all might be lost. The leaders might also feel that it was immoral to attack without adequate provocation even if they felt certain of a costless win, particularly if the opponent's missiles were located so close to his cities that an attack on the missiles would also destroy cities. Not only would an unprovoked attack by A be immoral, but killing millions of B's citizens could have all kinds of political aftereffects. Such aftereffects would probably be enhanced if A got away untouched, so that his likely argument—that the attack was preemptive, and therefore defensive—would not be plausible (even if it were right).

Given all of the above caveats, the balance of terror would still be unstable if A had, say, 2,100 missiles and B only had 1,000. A might then be unsophisticated or immoral enough to attack. Let us make the situation somewhat more stable by giving B an additional twenty missiles, but assume these last are completely reliable and invulnerable.[3] Now if A fires 2,000 of his 2,100 missiles at B's 1,020, he will destroy 1,000 of them all right, but B will still be able to fire back 20 missiles at A. This small fraction of B's original force would still kill 20 per cent of A's population. No modern nation has lost 20 per cent of its population in a war. In all but the most desperate circumstances, A is therefore likely to be deterred. In fact, about the only situation in which A might be provoked into an attack would be if B initiated a limited strategic strike as envisaged in the previous discussion. The deterrence is

[2] In the real world, damage is a complex phenomenon and the best way to render the other side's missiles ineffective may be to attack some of the system elements (see Kahn, *On Thermonuclear War*, pp. 128–30), such as command and control, or to damage by subtle weapons effects (see *ibid.*, pp. 428–33).
[3] The real-world analogue might be some very hard missiles or some that are very well concealed, perhaps by mobility; or one might think of the twenty missiles as being a sort of irreducible (2 per cent) survival from a well-executed attack.

not symmetrical. A might be willing to use limited strategic retaliation against B. Though it would be irrational for B to escalate to all-out war, A would still be taking an awful chance. B might react emotionally or stupidly with an all-out reprisal. However, most likely he would not. The certainty of a totally destructive reprisal is likely to deter him.

Of course, B might still have enough resolve to exact a full tit-for-tat retribution. If B were sufficiently ruthless or resolved, he might even try to exact more than just tit for tat in his reprisal, but for B to do this safely requires either some asymmetry in resolve, or a rather overly "reasonable" attitude on the part of A; however, it could happen.

In this situation, where A has 2,100 2-for-1 missiles and B has 1,000 vulnerable and 20 invulnerable missiles, A has another strategic option. He can conduct a low-level counterforce operation rather than a possibly ineffective show of force or an excessively provoking, even if limited, city attack. In these operations against B's missile force, A would presumably take care to do as little bonus damage as possible. He would then be signaling to B, "While I am being careful, I am clearly committed. It must be you who backs down. I can, if necessary, afford to go to the limit. You clearly cannot." Dangerous as this strategy may be for A, it is probably not as dangerous as a limited attack on B's cities or even an all-out attack that would guarantee the loss of twenty of A's cities to B's all-out retaliation. Although A is risking the loss of all of his cities if B acts irrationally, A might prefer to accept this risk rather than the certain loss of twenty cities.

Note that it will do B little good to retaliate with the same kind of limited counterforce attack, because he uses up two missiles in attack for every one he destroys, and thus just increases the rate at which his force is diminished. Such a retaliatory attack also increases A's relative military superiority, but this is irrelevant under the assumptions of our simple model.

The low-level controlled counterforce operation is particularly feasible if the missile and city target systems are separated—if, for example, B's cities have fall-out protection or his missiles are vulnerable to air burst and there is at least a moderate physical separation of missiles and cities. By making controlled counterforce operations less destructive, civil defense could make it less likely that there would be an escalation into all-out war or limited city-trading. Therefore, if B procures some modest civil defense, he may decrease his ability to deter A. In fact, in these circumstances A might be tempted to fire 2,000 of his missiles at B's 1,000 and thus create a situation in which A has 100 missiles and B has 20 missiles and both sides have 100 undamaged cities. It would now be more possible for A to conduct a controlled reprisal operation against B and still limit his risk. If worst comes to worst, B can only destroy twenty of A's cities. Cataclysmic as this would be, it would not be as cataclysmic as A's threat against B—total annihilation. While B may still win the "bargaining"—since neither side wishes to lose twenty cities and A might therefore back down before B—under most circumstances A should nevertheless be able to exploit, to some extent, the asymmetry in the threats.

A would have less of an advantage over B if he were unable to conduct his campaign in a short period of time. Assume, for example, that A can fire only ten missiles a day. Then A's campaign against B would take 200 days.[4] At any time during that campaign, B could initiate a controlled reprisal against A at, say, the rate of one city a day. If B's controlled reprisal were initiated in the first 100 days, then A would no longer have an advantage over B; so long as the exchange rate was "equitable," both would run out of cities before either ran out of missiles. If B were to initiate a campaign of controlled reprisal after 100 days, he would have to do so at a higher level (2 or 3 cities a day) or leave A with a bargaining advantage; at the 1 city per day rate, it is conceivable that B would run out of missiles before A ran out of cities and before either of them gave in.

Another complexity can be introduced by giving either A or B, or both, rural areas to which the city population can be evacuated. Let us assume also that there are adequate shelters in these rural areas so that the evacuees are invulnerable, but that neither A nor B will be able to recuperate unless each have at least ten cities surviving the war.

Both A and B now have a new tactic open to them; they can evacuate. Such an operation is at the same time less provocative than a show of force or a limited attack, and more menacing. It is not violent in itself, but it could be the prelude to either an all-out attack or a limited one. Neither A nor B would any longer be risking his people by attacking, but only his property. But the situation is not symmetrical; B's threat is somewhat illusory. If B attacks and destroys all of A's cities, A will destroy *all* of B's cities in reprisal and B will die a slow death rather than a fast one. Slow

or fast, B will still die. A, on the contrary, can attack B and expect to lose only twenty cities in B's retaliation. However, the situation is not as overwhelmingly one-sided as it might seem; the evacuation is still dangerous to A, for B may not understand that the loss of his cities will result in an inevitable slow death—indeed, it might take a good deal of analysis to convince him and there might not be time for the analysis. Of course A could pre-empt, but this might make inevitable the loss of twenty cities. Even if these cities were empty, A would probably prefer having his way peacefully to destroying B and losing twenty empty cities. In a more realistic example, there would also be those chilling uncertainties to give A pause before he made war inevitable—no matter how reassuring A's paper plans and calculations were.

The ability to evacuate would make all-out war look more feasible—correctly so to A, misleadingly so to B. It might also make controlled reprisal against cities more feasible; for, even though an evacuation would reduce the value of the cities as hostages and thus remove some of the sanctions against escalation, it also would make the controlled reprisal less provocative, since property alone, rather than people and property, would be destroyed. Perhaps even more importantly, it would provide a preliminary "moment of truth" for the decision-makers of both sides, during which they would be likely to divest themselves of many slogans and much humbug and think more clearly than they did before the evacuation about the risks of war and peace and what is vital and what is merely desirable.

The worst situation for B would occur if A had an evacuation ability and B

[4] The real-world analogue would be "peacetime" campaigns against Polaris submarines, or even carefully conducted campaigns of attrition directed against hidden or mobile missiles on land. Such campaigns might take months.

only had fallout protection in his cities. A could now evacuate and be in a very advantageous position to conduct a sanitary, controlled counterforce campaign. It would still be dangerous for A, especially if the counterforce campaign had to be long-drawn-out, as discussed in one of the previous examples; B could still threaten a controlled reprisal or an all-out attack on A's cities. This would not only threaten A's standard of living and his cultural and historical landmarks, but by hypothesis it would threaten his very survival. A's recuperation depends on his having at least ten cities survive the war. Another complication that would arise in any controlled reprisal against cities would be in "agreeing" on the equitable exchange rate between A's empty cities and B's populated cities. This complication might be overwhelming.

Let us consider another case. Assume that the missiles are so vulnerable, reliable, and dispersed that in a counterforce attack they trade evenly one for one. There would now be tremendous pressures toward an arms race, particularly if either side were uncertain as to how many missiles the other side had. The side with a few more missiles could launch a disarming first strike at the other side, and (in the simple model) then attack the other side's cities with impunity. Because a small difference in numbers might be vital, accurate intelligence is critically important. In its absence, the side that can preserve secrecy may bluff. For example, a side with less missiles might still start a low-level controlled counterforce campaign as if it expected to be able to destroy all of its opponent's missiles before it used up its own. Such action might make its claim to superiority very credible. Or it might cast doubt on it. If the attacker

was so superior, why didn't he go all out? However, there would be many reasons for his restraint and the question would remain open.

Let us now change the model again and assume that the missiles are clustered, so that one missile fired at the other side can take out two missiles. Now the situation is indeed unstable. By firing 500 missiles, either side can completely destroy the other side's forces and still have 500 missiles left over with which it can threaten or attack cities. Thus even though each side has a first-strike overkill capability against the other side's cities, neither will have an overkill in terms of the balance of terror, or indeed any second-strike (retaliatory) capability at all. As opposed to the first model, which we called "stable deterrence," this one could be called "unstable deterrence" (there will still be some deterrence). Because each side is likely to be anxious to get in the first blow if there is a war, both are likely to be trigger-happy and anything might set them off. However, in the real world there will always be those imponderables and moral and political questions; therefore, even though both sides greatly prefer a first strike to a second strike, both are still likely to prefer peace to war if there is a free choice between the two. Because the balance of terror is so unstable, both sides are likely to be wary (deterred) of provoking the other. Finally, if a provocative act seems necessary, one is likely to choose a disarming strike over the provocation, since it may seem less dangerous.

Let us now change this last model by giving each side twenty invulnerable missiles and also giving each side's cities enough fallout protection so that they will not be bonus targets in counterforce attacks. We now have a situation that could be called "multistable deterrence," in which both sides may symmetrically have adequate deterrence against both direct attack and provocation. If either side goes first, it can destroy 1,000 of its opponent's missiles by using only 500 missiles. It can thus reduce the other side to 20 missiles while retaining 520. Presumably it can use the subsequent imbalance to coerce its opponent into signing an acceptable peace treaty. If it cannot, it risks losing 20 per cent of its cities. It may have enough confidence in the likelihood that both its attack and the subsequent coercion will succeed for it to risk attacking if sufficiently provoked. It is also unlikely to be sufficiently certain that both the attack and the postattack coercion will work and therefore be unwilling to risk an attack except under the gravest provocation or extreme pressures.

Assume now that A has only 100 invulnerable missiles and that B has 50. One would then think that Side A could get the edge over Side B. This is, however, not necessarily so—much less so than if the balance were 100 to 20. If A starts a controlled reprisal in which each side loses a city a day, Side B is just about as likely as not to have more perseverance than Side A; long before the fiftieth day is reached, Side A may back down. While both sides will be conscious of the possibility that at the fiftieth day Side A will have a clear advantage, and this will somewhat encourage Side A and discourage Side B, this fact is not likely to dominate the bargaining—fifty cities is a lot to lose, and thus Side B probably has a considerable margin of deterrence.

Let us assume still another case. Assume that if Side A and Side B get into a war, their forces are mixed and not homogeneous, and the vulnerability varies. The situation is symmetrical and is such

that the side striking first can reduce the side that is attacked to 50 invulnerable missiles, while the attacker will have more than 100 invulnerable missiles left over. (How many more is irrelevant in our model.) We have now reduced the situation to one of the cases already considered. It is clear that while the side striking first will have a bargaining advantage over the side that was struck, the advantage will be even less than in the previous example, particularly if the war is conducted over a period of days. There is also the additional possibility that, long before it is reduced to fifty missiles, the losing side can start a controlled reprisal to try to induce the other side to quit the war under some terms or other.

SOME REAL COMPLICATIONS

Although it would be useful to go on generating simple models, we have probably gone far enough for the purposes of this paper. I have already emphasized that, helpful as such models are for developing language and concepts and clarifying elementary ideas, the ideas they illustrate must be explored systematically, critically, and in detail. Such details would include:

a. Who the enemy is.
b. When the war is fought.
c. Possible actions of other countries.
d. The equipment and postures of each side.
e. The plans and training of each side.
f. The way the war started.
g. The state of tension before the war.
h. Possible arms-control environment.
i. Political objectives, prewar and post-war.
j. Civil-defense status of both sides.

All of the above details, and others, must be considered in any realistic study, not only for the current status, but over the whole time period of interest.

To illustrate the point further, let us consider briefly some of the dynamic factors that would have to go into the substantive studies. In any particular instance—preattack or postattack—each side has a certain threat capability; that is, it can do a certain amount of counterforce damage and a certain amount of countervalue damage or varying combinations of these. (More counterforce damage will tend to mean less countervalue damage, and vice versa.) Furthermore, the notion of damage is complex. For example, in a counterforce attack by the United States against the Soviet Union, we might have as one objective Soviet advance bases in the northern part of the country, with the hope of frustrating the Soviets' immediate plans by making it temporarily difficult or impossible for their short-range medium bombers to use these bases for refueling. But this frustration may not be absolute. The Soviet Air Force could probably regroup, improvise, use aerial refueling, and do other things to recuperate its capability. A somewhat greater degree of damage, in the first strike or in subsequent waves, might hinder or permanently prevent this improvisation. Damage to command and control is obviously a critical factor, and yet hard to evaluate. Insofar as there are weapon carriers that are not destroyed (e.g., Polaris submarines and very hard missile sites and mobile missiles) and that do not need coordination in attacking, the major effect of destroying or degrading command and control would be a delay of the eventual order to fire, elimination of possible efficiencies available through retargeting, and added opportunity to coerce or intimidate the enemy, but the threat still looms. For bombers, some minimum command and control may be essential to provide coordination. Thus the concept of damage is a dynamic rather than a static concept; it can increase or decrease over time, by deterioration or recuperation.

When it comes to countervalue damage, the nation's decision-makers and their bargaining position will be affected by the amount of damage that has already been done as measured by the number of people killed, the property destroyed, whether this property has historical, cultural, or any other special values, and how badly the environment has already been affected. In most circumstances, the nation's leaders will be even more concerned with the enemy's threat, the people who may be killed, possible further potential reductions in the immediate postwar standard of living, and further degradation in the eventual capability to recuperate or the speed with which this recuperation can be carried out. The bargaining may also be affected if some portion of the country is considered to be relatively invulnerable. The decision-makers might be much affected by their estimate of what would be left in a last-ditch extremity—what is the ultimate threat the enemy can pose at any particular point. Finally, there are the physical, political, and emotional capabilities for command and control. The actual bargaining will be much affected by the state of information about both sides, such as each side's estimate of the other side's estimate, and vice versa—including estimates of the effects of attempts to bluff and otherwise mislead. Even seemingly trivial details, such as the exact relation between the timing of the attack and any ultimatum that may be delivered, or the form and language of this ultimatum, can also be important. It is exactly such details that can cause a decision-maker to be more or less rational, more or less resolved, more or less reckless.

These last considerations may be central. Each side may be more interested in using threats skillfully rather than missiles, since attacks on morale or resolve may be more effective in achieving objectives than the direct effect of physical damage.

It is the aim of each side to attempt to achieve some sort of bargain, and resolve may be more vulnerable than weapons. Attacks against resolve could use communication, persuasion techniques, misinformation, sabotage, espionage, and tactics designed to frighten and deter, while minimizing provocation that might lead to the "wrong" kind of emotional or irrational act. Or one might want so much to maximize apprehension that worries about provocation would be secondary. As a hypothetical example, imagine that one side spares its opponent's ten largest cities while destroying as many of the others as it is capable of doing. The side with only ten cities surviving might be easily intimidated by the prospect of losing the remainder. Having lost so much, it might feel (possibly correctly) that these last assets—the ten largest cities—would be essential to its recuperation. It might also be clear that its attacker had more than enough capability left to destroy these last ten cities. Creating this situation, in which all the opponent's remaining eggs are in a small number of baskets, might actually improve the attacker's bargaining position over a situation in which it had not destroyed any cities at all but had concentrated on destroying strategic forces. In other words, the importance of the assets visualized as being at risk as compared with the assets not at risk greatly influences the effectiveness of the enemy's threats.

Bargaining against the background of controlled reprisal is likely to be very simple, mostly in the form of "take it or leave it." There are, however, roughly six distinguishable classes of peace offers that might accompany such a war: (1) an unconditional surrender by the enemy; (2) concession of defeat by the enemy with acceptance of specific surrender terms and guarantees; (3) a cease-fire under current conditions; (4) a cease-fire with a return to the *status quo ante;* (5) a situation in which we concede defeat but demand guarantees and terms before agreeing to a cease-fire; and (6) an unconditional surrender on our part. One would not necessarily try to conduct such negotiations with the prewar government; one might try to divide the enemy—e.g., to negotiate with the military authorities or with some other powerful group. Exactly what might be done depends a lot on the timing and the prewar situation. This last may be particularly crucial. How the prewar crisis started and developed into a war could make all the difference—for example, in the many "moments of truth" provided by the prewar escalations, war plans may be re-examined and changed. In any case, decision-makers are likely to receive a lot of strategic education, while military leaders may have important and surprising constraints imposed on their plans.

All such bargaining is going to be complicated by mistaken information, communication difficulties, pressure of time, and finally the disturbing effect of emotions, irrationality, anger, miscalculation, bad doctrine, misapprehension, mistakes, and the like. At the upper end of an escalation ladder, some of these effects are likely to be greatly intensified.

Probably the highest-priority studies we need in this field are studies of the cost-effectiveness type, under various assumptions as to what constraints might be observed during the fighting and the relationship of these constraints to the probable stability of the process. These studies should include an analysis of the stability of certain thresholds and how they might change. If we are to be prepared for these remote but important possibilities, all of these things must be studied extensively and in detail and preparations made to influence them.

Sir Solly Zuckerman:

JUDGMENT AND CONTROL IN MODERN WARFARE

One of the originators of the method of "systems analysis" widely used by thermonuclear strategists, Sir Solly Zuckerman, developed that approach in Great Britain during World War II. Now scientific adviser to the Minister of Defense in Great Britain, he discusses in the article which follows the limitations of systems analysis, especially when— as in thermonuclear strategy—it cannot be based on any historical or experimental evidence about the use of the relevant weapons in battle.

THE trend of military evolution on which the world has been set since 1939 has seen the harnessing of the most advanced technology to the elaboration of an extensive series of new weapons and weapons systems. Through the development of a large family of ballistic and non-ballistic missiles, destructive power can now be brought to bear on unseen targets over distances ranging from tens to thousands of miles; at the same time, the capacity of a single explosion to destroy has been multiplied thousands, even millions, of times. These technological developments have been associated with the emergence of new scientific processes of management (most of which are loosely grouped under the term "operations analysis"), whose purpose is to try to help the commander control the apparatus of which he now disposes. But a question which becomes increasingly urgent in our age of nuclear deterrence, and one which grows in importance as more and more technology becomes harnessed to the demands of defense, is whether these new measures of control extend or curtail the possibilities of human, as opposed to machine, judgment.

A useful approach to an answer to the question is to consider three general propositions, of which one is observable fact and the other two are unassailable deductions from experience.

The observable fact is that the amount

From Sir Solly Zuckerman, "Judgment and Control in Modern War," *Foreign Affairs*, XL (January 1962), pp. 196–212. Copyright by the Council on Foreign Relations, Inc. Reprinted by permission.

of military input into modern weapons systems, and particularly complex strategic systems, is declining rapidly, with a complementary increase in the technical input provided by the non-military man. This change is associated with the increasing specialization of single-purpose weapons systems. By "military input" one means of course, the fruits of actual military experience. The simplest illustration of this proposition is that no military genius or experience has gone into the conception or design of I.C.B.M.s. If one wishes to push it that far, there is no logical need for such a weapon to be deployed by the military, as opposed to some other agent of government. If the name Moscow, or New York, or London, or Paris were written on each I.C.B.M., the missiles might well be deployed and operated by the firms which produced them. The complex operations of the U.S. National Aeronautics and Space Administration (NASA) are not military operations, nor is putting a man into space a military operation, even though the men who go into space may all be military men.

Sophisticated anti-aircraft missile systems are equally automatic in their conception—and, one suspects, in their potential operation. For them to operate properly, one needs virtually complete information about what is happening in one's air space, not to mention infallible and unshakeable judgment about what to do with that information.

My first major generalization, therefore, is that the more modern technology one puts into weapons systems, and the more automated they become, the less they constitute the fruits of military thinking, and the less flexible they become in use.

My second proposition is this: However much importance one attaches to fire-power, battles and wars are not necessarily won by matching unit powers of destruction, or by having a few more potential units of destruction than one's enemy. The best victory is the one where an adversary surrenders without a shot being fired; at the other extreme, the worst victory is one which is associated with a maximum of unnecessary and expensive destruction. War, of course, is a tricky game, and rather than take risks, commanders almost inevitably over-insure. Once there is no scarcity of bombs or aircraft, the tendency is to use more rather than fewer on a given task. The frequency with which the principle of economy of force has been violated in the past makes one wonder in what sense it constitutes a principle of real military action as opposed to something to talk about at staff colleges.

Space prevents my illustrating the proposition that neither battles nor wars are *uniquely* determined by matching units of destructive power. For present purposes, I base this assertion on an extensive series of special studies which I personally made of the "natural history" of destruction during the course of the 1939–1945 war. They all illustrate the conclusion that, while firepower is a major factor, it is only one of several vital factors which may determine the outcome of conflict. History, alas, provides no guide as to which factor will determine the outcome of some battle which has not yet been fought.

My third proposition is so obvious that it hardly bears mentioning. It is that the more vast, the more heterogeneous, the more scattered any organization becomes, and the more complicated its component parts—it makes no difference whether we consider the civil or the military sphere—the more difficult it is to control and to concert its multitudinous activities to a single common purpose. The difficulty is an ultimate limitation on the practical uses of good judgment.

II

Let us consider the first proposition—that in the present phase of military evolution military experience as such is contributing less and less to the development of complex weapons systems, and that, correspondingly, we are being committed more and more to systems which, as they grow more complex technologically than anything we could have conceived of before, increasingly limit our freedom of choice and action.

The nature of the military armory has always helped determine the character of tactics and strategy. To that extent, weapons have always set constraints on freedom of choice—which means on the exercise of judgment—when military means have been used to secure political ends. The danger today is that our complicated armory, and particularly our nuclear armory, may in the end drive us to a position in which we are committed to operate as in a set-piece. Such an eventuality would mean that if tactical warfare were ever to break out in Europe, it would simply become one part of a program of predetermined strategic action.

There is an immediate corollary to the overt recognition of this trend in weapons development. If the way in which our potential freedom of military operation and deployment is constrained becomes obvious—and in these expensive technological days these things cannot be kept secret in a democratic society—our potential enemies can adjust their plans, military and non-military, in a complementary way to suit their own convenience.

This trend in the development of tactical warfare as one part of a set-piece of predetermined strategic action may well be something we need as part of our strategic deterrence. But it is not what most people have in mind when they refer to the "proper use" of tactical nuclear weapons in a land battle in NATO Europe. It is essential, therefore, that the armory of which we dispose in order to defend ourselves in field warfare does not contain within itself tripwires which unwittingly set into operation the whole panoply of strategic deterrence. I know that this matter is very much the concern of General Norstad today. Ten years hence his successor will have to wrestle with an even more severe problem.

Let us be quite clear about this. There are those in the West who already believe that the use of any nuclear weapons in a war involving NATO would mean the opening of a Third World War. There are indications that the Soviet leaders believe the same thing. If this view is right, all freedom of choice may be lost, and with it all possibility of exercising judgment and control in a future war between the great powers.

I am not concerned here either to discuss this view or to paint the picture of mutual suicide which it entails. I refer to it simply as an indication of a major consequence of the development of weapons systems into which one builds only a predetermined set of functions. The guidance and navigational systems of a long-range ballistic missile are magnificent achievements, but they themselves are incapable of any more judgment than is built into them. Only in a very crude way is a nuclear-headed missile of this age a substitute for a manned aircraft. Once launched, all it substitutes for is the bomb the aircraft might have dropped.

The technological panoply of set-piece warfare is the panoply of deterrence. Its weapons are not weapons in the conventional sense. Our deterrent weapons are there to make any potential aggressor realize that if he strikes he will be struck. What would happen after that, in the case of strategic war, is matter for speculation, in which scientists have no need to engage in public. They may better appreciate the significance of the facts of destructive power, but they cannot lay claim to better imaginative powers than the next man.

There is one related point, however, that I must touch on. If one assumes that such a thing as tactical nuclear warfare could occur in isolation, how are armies equipped with nuclear weapons to be controlled? This is an immense problem for the military scientist. Only someone who wishes to blind himself to the obvious facts would fail to see that our machinery for surveillance and for condensing, analyzing, and disseminating military intelligence does not match the force and range of our striking power and the potential speed of reaction of the modern weapons systems which are deployed on the battlefield.

This is an enormously important area for military research and development. Which of several towns, or how many of them, are going to be effaced from the map as interdiction targets 50 or 100 miles from the front? More important, how is one to know what the effects of their elimination are on the movement of the enemy forces? Once our own nuclear weapons start detonating, how is the news of what is happening to be flashed from one to another part of our own lines? How are we to inform ourselves of what the enemy has done with his nuclear weapons? How are all these data to be collected? And, every bit as important, how are they to be reduced quickly enough to the kind of intelligible terms in which they could be disseminated and without which neither judgment nor control can be exercised?

III

I turn now to my second proposition, which is simply that battles and wars are not necessarily won by the side with the greater number of units of destruction at its disposal. A corollary of this proposition is that the way our power to destroy has multiplied over the past 15 years may itself impose a major limitation on military freedom of action in field warfare.

I do not propose to set out figures which define the nature of modern destructive power. The yield of the two bombs which destroyed Hiroshima and Nagasaki—two moderate-sized industrialized towns—was between 15 and 20 kilotons. The NATO armory contains weapons of this caliber, and also many others with higher and lower yields. The use of any one of these—and of any equivalent nuclear weapons the Russians might use—would mean the instantaneous and total destruction or elimination of an area varying in size between, say, a large village and a large town. Depending on the way forces are disposed, the explosion of a nuclear weapon of, say, 100 kilotons could mean the elimination of one or of dozens of battle groups or of one or of several squadrons of aircraft on the ground. But if one's target information happened to be wrong, it could mean the elimination of none.

The dispersal of troops, which is a tactical consequence of the power of nuclear weapons, is one of the basic reasons why we need a better apparatus than we now possess for the reconnaissance and surveillance of potentially nuclear battlefields, and why we also need better communications. It is a reason for increased mobility of troops, since this is as much a requirement of a nuclear battle—assuming such a thing is a reality—as of a conventional battle.

There is also the problem of radio-biological hazards, which again focuses attention sharply on the need for highly sophisticated intelligence and communications systems, if any measure of control is to be exercised under conditions of chaos.

When I use the term "chaos," I am thinking not only of the direct effects of radiation and blast resulting from attacks on purely military targets, but also of the likely effects on military operations of nuclear explosions on adjacent civilian populations. For, to the best of my knowledge, there is no area in Western Europe where a nuclear battle could be fought without causing considerable damage to non-military targets.

This point can be illustrated by what is a representative scenario of such a battle, but one smaller and more confined than most that have been considered. In a war game involving just three NATO Corps, nuclear weapons were "used" against military targets only, in an area of 10,000 square miles which contained no large towns or cities. In this "battle," lasting only a few days, it was assumed that the two sides together used a total of between 20 and 25 megatons in not fewer than 500 and not more than 1,000 strikes. It turned out that 3½ million people would have had their homes destroyed if the weapons were air burst, and 1½ million if ground burst. In the former case, at least half the people concerned would have been fatally or seriously injured. In the case of ground burst weapons, all 1½ mil-

lion would have been exposed to a lethal radiological hazard and a further 5 million to serious danger from radiation.

I am, as I have said, referring only to the actual battle area in which the three Corps were engaged. If we wish to obtain a more realistic impression of the circumstances which would actually prevail in such a limited battle, we need to bear in mind that no such operation, however confined, would be likely to occur without collateral, so-called interdiction attacks with nuclear weapons beyond the area of local engagement. Also, in all probability both sides would launch nuclear attacks on distant airfields or missile sites.

My purpose in trying to give an indication of some of the likely facts of a nuclear land battle—and I have described only part of the picture—is both to answer questions that have been put and to indicate that problems of judgment and control become increasingly difficult the more one's weapons automatically lead to over-hitting—even of strictly military targets.

In the ideal, the best weapon is the one just big enough to destroy the specific target against which it is directed. This is true whether looked upon from the standpoint of military practicality or plain economics. For example, both theoretical and field studies of World War II battles have shown that the smaller the units into which a given weight of anti-personnel weapons was divided, the greater the number of casualties they caused.

But nuclear weapons have changed all this. It will require the utmost judgment and control if the secondary, non-military effects—even when they are directed against assumed military targets—are not to dominate the situation once they are used, and having done so, to generate a new situation which is outside all possible military control, as it certainly now is outside all military experience. I am not suggesting that the problem of trying to operate rationally within an environment of chaos is new to military experience and command, or that civilian populations have not suffered from military operations in the past. What I am saying is that the problem today assumes such new proportions that it moves into a dimension completely different from the one in which we have all gained our experience.

There is, of course, no rule which says that a land battle in Europe would immediately "go nuclear." Equally, there is none which says that it would not. My experience of the way commanders worked in the Second World War does not lead me to suppose that, if unlimited force were available, less rather than more would be used in order to secure some objective, whether on the defensive or offensive.

The very existence of tactical nuclear weapons is thus the most urgent challenge that has ever been presented to military judgment and control. As weapons to deter aggression, they serve a very precise purpose; the context of field warfare in which they might actually be used is an entirely different matter. There can be very few military targets which are not disproportionately small in relation to the area of effect of the smallest nuclear weapon that might be used against them. Once one goes beyond, say, a yield of 20 kilotons, one is in the "town-elimination range." Because of this, one cannot make any valid comparisons between the introduction to the military scene of nuclear weapons and, say, the introduction of conventional explosives or chemical warfare at the time they emerged.

One further point. In the development of nuclear warheads, particularly those which are designed for missiles, there is a tendency to add to their yield in order to compensate for the inaccuracy of the delivery system and for inadequacies of target information. To a lesser extent, this is also true of free-falling and guided bombs. This, again, means that one builds into nuclear weapons greater destructive power than is necessary for military purposes, and that their secondary, non-military effects overshadow those which relate specifically to their military use.

IV

I turn now briefly to the third consideration which I see circumscribing the area within which military judgment and control can be exercised in this rapidly expanding technological age. It is simply that the larger, the more heterogeneous, the more complex, the more scattered any organization becomes, the more difficult it is to control its actions to fulfill a common purpose.

With active concurrence of the military, we have moved into an era of weapons systems rather than isolated weapons, and this trend is unlikely to be interrupted. Each new system emerges as a combination of complex components; and each of these needs to be monitored and manned in an increasingly specialized way. Early warning systems, missile systems, certain forms of intelligence systems—they are all similar in that each cog is vital, each has to be complete and perfect within itself, each has to have its built-in programs, computers and comparators. Each sub-system has to synchronize precisely with the next one. Increasing specialization of systems inevitably leads to rigidity of operation—and to the danger of breakdown.

Similarly, the men who operate and service the components of the newer weapons systems, whether they be early warning radar chains or supersonic high-altitude aircraft or Polaris submarines, are working at the extremes of their physical, psychological and mental capacities. As the decade progresses, each new weapons system will place still greater demands on the judgment and control of the individual.

Today, command has to be exercised over varieties of weapons systems which interlock over vast areas and, in the case of NATO, over systems which cross national frontiers. If the ultimate limitations of human judgment and control are not to be exceeded, it is vital that every effort be made to unify and simplify those human procedures which are concerned with the collection, interpretation, and dissemination of intelligence.

In examining the impact of future scientific developments on military affairs, there are two more points which I believe to be highly important. The first is that, while the sheer pressures created by technological progress themselves generate limitations to the proper and free exercise of judgment and control, the problem of maintaining this essential quality has not been made any easier by the way the military have altered the concrete nature of certain military problems by turning them into abstractions. One dangerous example of this tendency is the term "interdiction targets." Another is the idea that nuclear weapons are just a new and more powerful form of artillery, and that one exchanges "nuclear fire" like counter-battery fire. A third is that one is able "to restore a situation" with nuclear fire. There are other conventional military terms which relate properly to the pattern of warfare in pre-atomic days but

which hardly fit our present technological era.

We think we know what we mean when we use such terms as "interdiction." To take a special case, let us assume a series of bridges over a river; they must be destroyed lest they be used by the enemy, even though, as is so often the case, they are in centers of population. The nodal points in a railway communications network might be another set of interdiction targets. As such, they would be dealt with as part of a set-piece offensive.

In this kind of thinking, however, the target is not a body of troops or a particular bridge. It has become an abstraction— "interdiction." The purpose of interdicting—in this case, the prevention of the movement of a particular body of men—may not be fulfilled at all in "set-piece interdiction." For all we know, the men may not have been there, or may have planned to move by another route. This is how it often was in the Second World War with one major class of interdiction targets in Northwestern Europe; and I know nothing which suggests to me that it would not be the same in the next. The use of nuclear weapons to carry out interdiction plans may or may not impede the enemy, but it is very likely to make the environment more difficult for our own commanders to exercise judgment and control.

It seems to me, therefore, that when we talk about the potential use and effects of nuclear weapons, we must avoid the conceptual framework derived from the military terminology of prenuclear warfare. One may fairly ask what meaning there is to the idea of using nuclear weapons "to defend our territories and peoples." One can deter with nuclear weapons. Can one defend?

v

My final point derives from the fact that the situations encountered in warfare are as empirical and as experimental as those thrown up in a laboratory, and that they do not lend themselves any better to predetermined judgments. Experience in dealing with experimental situations helps one in dealing with new ones; but the results of one set of experiments do not apply to another—unless they are identical, which is seldom the case.

Warfare, the behavior of men and nations in conflict, is a far more complex thing than the behavior of men and women in normal peaceful groupings. Experience has shown that even the latter is hardly amenable to the discipline of scientific method. History, we know, was made yesterday; and social science has not yet provided the predictive generalizations which would allow us to write tomorrow's history today.

Discussion of this point requires a consideration of military operational analysis and how it was born—or perhaps I should say, was allowed to be born—in the Second World War. It emerged as a new procedure in military affairs, as an intellectual tool for the military, so as to help the proper exercise of judgment and control. Without it, warfare was already becoming too difficult technically for those in whose hands its conduct rested. I say this with no disrespect. In the American Civil War, in the Franco-Prussian War, in the First World War, war—in the words of Colonel Nathan Forrest—was still largely a matter of getting there "fustest with the mostest." Firepower had increased over the years both in range and in the degree of physical destruction that could be caused. The tank had increased the possibilities of mobility in the face of enemy fire. Chemical warfare, in spite of its limitations, was a clear-cut and understandable procedure that nearly broke the static conditions of trench warfare. In general, the strategists and tacticians of the First World War were still operating with weapons they could understand over ranges they could, in effect, see, and in accordance with the hallowed military principle of the economy of force.

With one minor qualification, the First World War was thus historically still a period of balanced military forces and balanced weapons systems. The balance lay essentially in the control the commander could exercise over his troops and weapons, the consequences of whose use were also within his comprehension, and potentially, therefore, within his control. I can see no other possible useful meaning to the term "balanced military force."

My one qualification to this generalization was the emergence of air warfare. This was the germ which destroyed the traditional frame in which the military commander had hitherto exercised his judgment and control. Out of the first aircraft grew a weapons system whose striking power was to leap well ahead of the capacity to apply destructive force specifically for the elimination of what it is still both useful and wise to call "military targets." The aircraft was thus as much a leap into the dark as into the air.

In comparison, the submarine, when it first appeared, was a weapon whose effects could be envisaged without difficulty. Submarines certainly imposed a new threat, but it was one which was understandable and technically manageable, given a detection system, depth charges, and the intelligent deployment of surface shipping and anti-submarine forces. In its traditional sense, it was—I use the word "was" deliberately, for it is different now that submarines have become launching platforms for ballistic missiles—a weapons system which was posed against specific but mobile targets. The aircraft was something quite different. Able to penetrate deeply into enemy territory, it could achieve effects the consequences of which were unpredictable, and certainly outside the framework of the airman's experience.

I do not know how it was in other countries, but we in Britain—to illustrate my point—entered the 1939–1945 war with highly unrealistic estimates of the capacity of aircraft to find their targets, and of the destructive power of the bombs they dropped. Equally, we either underestimated or overestimated the resilience of people under attack, or the economic consequences of our strategic attacks, or the functional significance of different target systems. We had to learn the hard way. We had to learn to treat air operations as an empirical experience, the results of which had to be analyzed with a strict respect for scientific discipline if the next set of plans was not to perpetuate the errors of those preceding it. Because the results of our air plans were not analyzed in this way during the first half or so of the war, at the start they did, in fact, often merely perpetuate errors. Submarine warfare, too—on the scale it was waged during World War II—became a matter for analysis of a kind different from what had gone before. In short, war was becoming extremely complicated technically. Scientific analysis, in consequence, became as powerful an intellectual tool as the more traditional kinds of military intelligence. And sometimes it was far more valuable and reliable.

Operational analysis was thus born out of the need generated by the inter-action of a variety of complex problems resulting from the intrusion of modern technology into the military environment. In essence, and at its simplest, it was no different from the methods by which industry had improved its operations over the years. It came late into the military sphere, because the military world until then was a more conventional world, one less amenable to directional change than the continuously competitive world of commerce and trade. Then three varieties of operational research emerged.

The first category can be described as the analysis—observational and experimental—of the technical and military problems relating to the introduction of new weapons and techniques. The advent of radar is the classic example of this category of operational research. If radar was going to work, civilian scientists had to be brought into the military machine. And if the civilians were to discover how to work radar, they had to become operational researchers, or operations analysts, in order to see how the new apparatus could be fitted into a military context. Other examples of this category of operational research can be found in the field of electronic countermeasures and in the logistics of supply.

The second category of operational research dealt with the tactical consequences of the interaction of new and complex weapons systems and technologies. It concerned itself with the scientific appraisal of new situations in warfare resulting from the threat imposed by these weapons systems. Anti-submarine warfare is the classic example of this kind of operational analysis.

The third category of operational research consisted in the analysis of the way military plans—both strategic and tactical—unfolded in actuality, as opposed to how they were supposed to work. It was in this kind of operational analysis that I was particularly interested, and which I had the opportunity to develop as a result of my association first with Admiral Mountbatten, at that time Chief of Combined Operations in the United Kingdom, later with General Norstad, then on the staff of General Spaatz in the Mediterranean Area, and then with Air Chief Marshal Tedder in northwestern Europe.

No opportunity of analyzing operations in relation to their stated purpose was afforded us until early 1943, when the Axis forces were driven out of the Western Desert and North Africa. As the British armies advanced, studies were made of Tripoli and of other targets of air operations. The bomb damage as seen on the ground, and as recorded by the civil authorities at the time, was compared with the operational planning of, and intelligence reports on, the attacks which had caused the damage.

Essentially, what was being done was to treat each operation as one might an experiment of a very crude kind. How closely did what was achieved correspond to what we had set out to do? Why were intention and effect not always the same? A much more direct experimental approach was followed in planning and in executing the operations which led to the capture of the island of Pantellaria in 1943 and in analyzing them afterward—work in which I was closely associated with General Norstad. The lessons learned from this operation were then applied in 1944 to the pre-D-Day offensive against the coastal defenses of northern France. Similarly, the lessons learned from a detailed analysis of the functional effects of attacks on the railway system of Sicily and southern Italy provided the basis for the 1944

plan to destroy the communications network of northwestern Europe. Subsequent analysis fully confirmed all the expectations that had been based on the experience gained in the Mediterranean. However, there was little opportunity for this kind of analysis of field warfare—largely, I think, because it moved too fast for the results, when they became available, to be applied; also, the situations in field warfare were infinitely more varied than in either air or sea war.

I am emphasizing this aspect of operational research because its purpose is also that of the new school of operational analysis which is trying to achieve its objectives by theoretical and abstract reasoning, aided by recourse to various mathematical treatments of the concept of probability.

But before I discuss this new aspect of modern operational analysis, let me refer to another and simpler postwar variant of operational research as it applies in the military field. This is the kind of systems operations analysis that is carried out before one starts developing a weapons system for some definable purpose. It considers the operation of component sub-systems not only within themselves but also in their relation to other subsystems. For example, a sophisticated air-defense system requires ground radar and associated data-handling systems. It needs command links. And these in turn have to be tied in with the active or passive elements which are deployed to deal with the actual attack.

Obviously, the only thing that matters is: "Can the whole system deal with the attack?" If the strike component of the defense is too slow, it does not matter how efficient the radar system is— and so on. Within the limitations imposed by such factors as range and response time, extent of cover, and—dare one say it?—financial cost and lead time, each part of the whole must be designed for optimum efficiency in order to achieve one end result.

Compared to what goes on in an actual battle, this should be a relatively simple problem for the operational analyst. The requirements seem precise enough; the parameters in the equations seem measurable; everything is as it should be for the mathematical and statistical analysis of an extremely complicated situation. In fact, one cannot do without this kind of extrapolated, theoretical operations analysis. But let us be honest with ourselves. The number of times this kind of systems analysis has come up with the wrong answers—by which I mean encouraged the development of the wrong systems—provides a warning that theoretical operational analysis is only an aid to, and not a substitute for, human judgment.

VI

Now let me turn to the more abstract form of operational analysis which has emerged over the postwar years. It deals with what has been called "the mathematizing of thought processes," and is based upon "game theory," which burst upon the world a few years ago. Protagonists believe that this form of operational analysis can contribute materially to "decision making" in the fields of strategy and tactics. The issues with which it deals, then, are among the most important which face Western man today—deterrent strategy and nuclear warfare in particular. Upon its conslusions—so we are told—are based certain of the most important decisions which have been taken in determining the defense posture of the United States in the strategic field, as well as some of the prede-termined decisions which would be taken if deterrence ever failed.

I do not pretend to understand the intricacies of either the mathematics or the logical symbolism one finds in the writing of the game theorists. As I understand it, game theory is based upon the interaction of sequences of probabilities. It is assumed—to oversimplify the basic case—that you can calculate from a move made by an opponent at chess which of several possible moves open to you is the best—and so on to victory. In the next remove, it is assumed that you can make this best choice even when one randomizes one's opponent's moves. As a result, decision makers, we are told, can "optimize their solutions" even in the most complicated situations. This should undoubtedly be true in some cases—at any rate in theory—for example, in such problems as choosing where best to build a road, or which of several ways is the cheapest and best to build a nuclear reactor of a given type.

Certain parts of the very wide areas with which the calculations of the strategic game theorists deal are undoubtedly amenable to the most rigid treatment by formal logic and by means of probability statistics or mathematics, and the conclusions which emerge are fully valid over the part of the field to which they relate. What worries me is the fact that the total situation with which the theorists deal also contains extremely broad parameters of so qualitative a nature that no one could attribute numerical values to them. Some of these parameters are among the most important issues with which the game-theory strategists pretend to deal—if not the most important. For example, they include such matters as the enemy's intentions, as well as his strength and capacity; the resolution of our people; the capacity of a country to restore itself economically when it has suffered a degree of devastation well beyond anything that lies within human comprehension— let along experience—and other matters equally vague. These are vitally important issues. But they are not numerical issues, and probably never could be made such, even if they were ever to come within our experience.

I have already said that some of the more empirical results of the analysis of operational planning in the Second World War were subsequently used in the planning of new operations. What I did not say was that this took place only after considerable energy had been spent in persuading people that what had happened had indeed happened, and that experience was as useful a basis for the elaboration of future plans as was wishful thinking. Since this was so 20 years ago in a less rapidly moving technological age, what I, as a scientist, would like to know now is what weight would a commander really attach—when the moment of decision came—to the new kind of abstract operational analysis as an aid to his judgment?

Mathematical conceptions of probability clearly have real value in experimental situations when they relate to precise issues. But the more qualitative and non-numerical—the more human—the factors that are played into the system, the less precise and, indeed, the less meaningful become the estimates of probability that are churned out of the machine. One has to remember, too, that the social and political significance and weight of the different qualitative factors concerned in these strategic situations vary not only between themselves but also from moment to moment. Strategy, no more than politics, can be static.

The fact that the considerations of the new school of operational analysis do not violate the laws of physics or engineering seems unimportant to me. What is important is that, if our sophisticated preparations for possible tactical warfare link the latter more closely with the set-piece strategic deterrent, game-theory operational analysis may not be able to help the tactical commander in his hour of need. As I have said, estimates of probability become less valuable the less precise numerically the matters with which they deal become. Can this kind of operational analysis serve any purpose at all in the field of military judgment and command? Does it now? Can it ten years hence? These are vital questions to which commanders should— so it seems to me—address themselves.

I believe that some commanders are over-optimistic, and over-generous, in what they imply about the scientific nature of the social sciences. I know of no philosopher of science, no student of scientific method, who would claim that the generalizations of the social sciences could ever be characterized by the same attributes of predictive value which apply to the natural sciences. The processes of war are essentially sociological phenomena—and like other such phenomena they certainly do not constitute the material out of which one can yet see a predictive science being born. It is conceivable that it might become such one day—as conceivable as the idea that "the thought processes can be mathematized." But if this involves, as I imagine it must, a prior understanding of the biochemical and biophysical nature of thought processes, that day is far away.

The validity of probability methods when applied to single events is an academic matter which has not yet been sorted out. The conclusions of the new school of theoretical military analysis are in essence based upon probability laws which apply to repetitive situations. If one decides wrongly about the use of nuclear weapons, we shall be in a situation which may never repeat itself, which may end the leadership of the Western world—win or lose—in one critical shot.

Before game theory burst upon a too-generous military world, Whitehead, a world-renowned philosopher and mathematician, had written:

There is a curious misconception that somehow the mathematical mysteries of statistics help us to evade the proper limitations of the observed past. But statistics tell you nothing about the future unless you make the assumption of the permanence of statistical form. . . . Mathematics can tell you the consequences of your beliefs. For example, if your apple is composed of a finite number of atoms, mathematics will tell you that the number is odd or even. But you must not ask mathematics to provide you with the apple, the atoms, and the finiteness of their number. There is no valid inference from mere possibility to matter of fact, or in other words, from mere mathematics to concrete nature.

If ever there was a world in which situations do not repeat themselves like some mass production model, it is the military world. If we are to avoid the imposition of arbitrary limits to the exercise of judgment and control, let us be careful not to create in a mathematical vacuum situations which are based neither on past experience of affairs, nor on any conception of the innumerable variables and factors that determine social decision either today or tomorrow. The human brain, human values, human judgments, are still superior to the mechanics and processes of electronic computers or guidance systems. The day this ceases to be true there will probably be no human brains. But until then, let us use true scientific method as an aid to human judgment— and not as a hindrance. Science *is* human experience; it is not an alternative to judgment, and it is certainly not something that can operate outside human experience.

Robert S. McNamara:

THE DAMAGE-LIMITING
STRATEGY

*Robert S. McNamara was appointed Secretary of Defense by Presi-
dent Kennedy, after a career as super-manager for the Ford Company.
In the Defense Department he has applied business-managerial techniques for analyzing the cost and effectiveness of alternative approaches
to weapons systems and strategies. Here he discusses the changes occurring in America's military posture during his first three years in the
Pentagon, and explains the "damage-limiting strategy"—a particular
variant of controlled thermonuclear war—which became the dominant
American strategy during those three years.*

BEFORE long this Administration will
be presenting, once again, the details of a proposed national defense
budget for the consideration of the Congress and the public. Given the importance of these matters, their complexities
and uncertainties and the existence of
real differences of opinion, a degree of
controversy is inevitable, and even desirable.

Some controversies, however, reveal
underlying differences in perspective
that scarcely suggest the participants are
living in the same world.

Within the past few weeks, some critics have suggested that we have literally hundreds of times more strength than
we need; others have accused us of
risking the whole future of the nation
by engaging in unilateral disarmament. I
would like to believe that criticisms
bracketing our policy in that fashion
prove it to be rational and sound. But a
discrepancy of that order cannot be
reassuring. Rather, it indicates that we

have failed to convey to some part of
our audience even the broadest outlines,
as we see them, of the problems that our
military strategy and force structure are
meant to address. I believe we should be
able to move from controversy on that
scale toward consensus in military affairs,
not always on details or components of
our policies, but at least on an apprecia-
tion of the major national security problems confronting us, on the broad alternative paths to their solution, and on the
dominant goals, obstacles, costs, and
risks affecting choice. My purpose in
speaking to you this evening is to help
move in this direction.

As a prelude, then, to the coming season of debate, I should like to identify
and discuss some basic matters on which
a considerable degree of consensus
seems to me both possible and desirable,
although by no means assured.

These include those over-all comparative strengths and weaknesses of the opposing military alliances that form the

From Robert S. McNamara, "The Damage-Limiting Strategy." Remarks before the Economic Club
of New York, November 18, 1963.

bold relief in the strategic environment. In short, they are the considerations that seem to have relatively long-term significance compared to the annual budget cycle.

Matters of that degree of permanence tend to be stamped on our minds as being unchanging and unchangeable, the unquestioned framework of daily and yearly policy-making. Yet these factors of which I shall speak do change: more swiftly and more profoundly than our picture of them tends to change. Indeed, I believe it is just the fact that over the last decade this topography has changed—while many maps have not—that accounts for some apparently irreconcilable controversies.

Let me recall the earlier period briefly, for comparison. The strategic landscape at the outset of the 'Fifties was dominated by two outstanding features. One was the practical U.S. monopoly of deliverable, strategic nuclear weapons. The other was the Soviet Union and Communist China's virtual monopoly of ground force on the continents of Europe and Asia.

Both of these determinants of Western military policy had changed considerably by the end of the Korean War. The Soviets had produced atomic explosions and had created a sizable nuclear delivery capability against Europe, while NATO ground forces had expanded rapidly, and military operations in Korea had greatly tarnished the significance of Chinese Communist superiority in numbers. But the old notions of monopoly persisted as short-cut aids to thinking on policy matters. And they were not so misleading as they came later to be. Soviet armed forces approaching five million men still heavily outweighed the NATO forces in Europe; and Soviet delivery capability against the U.S. was dwarfed by that of SAC. Moreover, tactical nuclear weapons were being heralded as a new nuclear monopoly for the West.

Even as these earlier notions of monopolies grew obsolete, ideas about the feasibility of alternative policies continued to reflect them. So did ideas about how wars might be fought. Nuclear operations, both strategic and tactical, by the U.S. in response to Soviet aggression against our allies were considered to be virtually unilateral. Hence it was supposed the problem of credibility of the U.S. response would scarcely arise, even in the case of relatively limited Soviet aggressions. Western reliance upon nuclear weapons, in particular strategic systems, both to deter and to oppose non-nuclear attack of any size seemed not only adequate but also unique in its adequacy.

That sort of situation is convenient for policy-makers. It makes policy easy to choose and easy to explain. Perhaps that is why throughout most of the 'Fifties, while the Soviets under various pressures decreased their ground forces and the NATO allies built theirs up, and while the Soviets acquired a massive nuclear threat against Europe and laid the groundwork for a sizable threat against the U.S., the picture underlying most policy debate remained that appropriate to 1949. It was a picture of a Communist Goliath in conventional strength facing a Western David, almost naked of conventional arms but alone possessed of a nuclear sling.

Toward the end of that decade, the prospect that the Soviets would acquire intercontinental ballistic missiles at a time when our strategic forces consisted almost entirely of bombers focused our attention and our budget even more sharply than before upon our strategic forces. The urgency of the problem of deterring the most massive of attacks was a new reason for thinking that the West could spare neither resources nor thought to deal more specifically with lesser threats. The most urgent task was to provide for deterrence of massive aggression by assuring the survival under any attack of forces at least adequate, in the calculations of a potential attacker, to destroy his society in retaliation. It was now not the assurance of continued nuclear superiority that preempted the attention of policy-makers but, on the contrary, the struggle to maintain it.

But it is time for the maps to change by which policy is charted and justified. The old ones, which assumed a U.S. nuclear monopoly, both strategic and tactical, and a Communist monopoly of ground combat strength, are too far removed from reality to serve as even rough guides.

Neither we nor our allies can afford the crudities of maps that tell us that old policies are still forced upon us, when a true picture would show important new avenues of necessity and choice.

What most needs changing is a picture of ourselves and of the Western Alliance as essentially at bay, outmanned and outgunned except for nuclear arms no longer exclusively ours. We should not think of ourselves as forced by limitations of resources to rely upon strategies of desperation and threats of vast mutual destruction, compelled to deal only with the most massive and immediate challenges, letting lesser ones go by default. It would be a striking historical phenomenon if that self-image should be justified. We are the largest member of an Alliance with a population of almost 450 million people, an aggregate annual product which is fast approaching a tril-

lion dollars, and a modern and diverse technological base without parallel, facing the Soviet Union and its European satellites with their hundred million fewer people and an aggregate output no more than half that of the West.

And quite apart from ignoring the underlying strengths of the West, the outdated picture I have described takes no account of the military capabilities in being that our investment over the last decade, and specifically in the last few years, have bought for us. If new problems put strong claims on our attention and our resources today, it is very largely because we have come a large part of the way that is feasible toward solving some old ones.

Let me summarize the current status of the balance of strategic nuclear forces, that part of the military environment that has preoccupied our attention for so long. In strictly relative numerical terms, the situation is the familiar one. The U.S. force now contains more than 500 operational long-range ballistic missiles—Atlas, Titan, Minuteman, Polaris —and is planned to increase to over 1700 by 1966. There is no doubt in our minds and none in the minds of the Soviets that these missiles can penetrate to their targets. In addition, the U.S. has Strategic Air Command bombers on air alert and over 500 bombers on quick reaction ground alert. By comparison, the consensus is that today the Soviets could place about half as many bombers over North America on a first strike. The Soviets are estimated to have today only a fraction as many intercontinental missiles as we do. Furthermore, their submarine-launched ballistic missiles are short range, and generally are not comparable to our Polaris force. The Soviets pose a very large threat against Europe, including hundreds of intermediate and medium-range ballistic missiles. This threat is today and will continue to be covered by the clear superiority of our strategic forces.

The most wishful of Soviet planners would have to calculate as a certainty that the most effective surprise attack they could launch would still leave us with the capability to destroy the attacker's society. What is equally pertinent is that the relative numbers and survivability of U.S. strategic forces would permit us to retaliate against all the urgent Soviet military targets that are subject to attack, thus contributing to the limitation of damage to ourselves and our allies.

Deterrence of deliberate, calculated attack seems as well assured as it can be, and the damage-limiting capability of our numerically superior forces is, I believe, well worth its incremental cost. It is a capability to which the smaller forces of the Soviet Union could not realistically aspire. That is one reason, among others, why I would not trade our strategic posture for that of the Soviets at any point during the coming decade.

But given the kind of force that the Soviets are building, including submarine-launched missiles beyond the reach of our offensive forces, the damage which the Soviets could inflict on us and our allies, no matter what we do to limit it, remains extremely high.

That has been true for our allies ever since the middle and late 'Fifties. Soviet acquisition of a sizable delivery capability against the U.S., and more significantly their acquisition of relatively protected forces, submarine-launched or hardened, has been long and often prematurely heralded. Its arrival at last merely dramatizes the need to recognize that strategic nuclear war would under all foreseeable circumstances be bilateral—and highly destructive to both sides.

Larger budgets for U.S. strategic forces would not change that fact. They could have only a decreasing incremental effect in limiting somewhat the damage that the U.S. and its allies could suffer in a general nuclear war. In short, we cannot buy the capability to make a strategic bombing campaign once again a unilateral prospect.

That must, I suggest, be accepted as one of the determinants affecting policy. Another is that the same situation confronts the Soviet leaders, in a way that is even more intensely confining. In fact, enormous increases in Soviet budgets would be required for them to achieve any significant degree of damage-limiting capability. The present Soviet leaders show no tendency to challenge the basis of the U.S. strategic deterrent posture by such expenditures.

In the last two years alone, we have increased the number of nuclear warheads in the strategic alert forces by 100 per cent. During that period we have more than doubled the megatonnage of the strategic alert forces. The fact that further increases in strategic force size will at last encounter rapidly diminishing returns—which is largely an effect of the very large investments the U.S. has made in this area—should be reflected in future budgets. The funding for the initial introduction of missiles into our forces is nearing completion. We can anticipate that the annual expenditure on strategic forces will drop substantially, and level off well below the present rate of spending. This is not to rule out the possibility that research now in progress on possible new technological developments, including the possibility of useful ballistic missile defenses, will require major new expenditures. In any event, there will be recurring costs of modernization.

In the field of tactical nuclear weapons, the picture is in important respects similar. The U.S. at present has in stockpile or planned for stockpile tens of thousands of nuclear explosives for tactical use on the battlefield, in anti-submarine warfare, and against aircraft. They include warheads for artillery, battlefield missiles, demolition munitions, bombs, depth charges, air-to-air missiles, and surface-to-air missiles. The consensus is that the U.S. is presently substantially superior in design, diversity, and numbers in this class of weapons.

This is an indispensable superiority, as we can readily understand if we consider how our problems of strategic choice would be altered if the tables were reversed and it were the Soviet Union which held a commanding lead in this field. Nevertheless, what we have is superiority, not monopoly, and even if tactical nuclear warfare can be limited, below some ill-defined threshold of strategic exchange, the key fact is that if the West initiates such warfare in the future it must be expected to be bilateral, in any theater which engaged the Soviet Union. Again, we cannot buy back a monopoly, or the assurance of unilateral use.

Finally, there is the area of what we call our general purpose forces. Within the last two years, we have increased the number of our combat-ready Army divisions by about 45 per cent, from 11 to 16. There has been a 30 per cent increase in the number of tactical air squadrons; a 75 per cent increase in airlift capabilities; and a 100 per cent increase in ship construction and conversion to modernize the fleet.

But it is not only force size that matters. The key to the effective utilization of these forces is combat readiness and mobility.

The most recent demonstration of our ability to reinforce our troops presently stationed in Europe occurred last month in Operation Big Lift, the first of a series of planned large-scale, world-wide exercises. For the first time in military history, an entire division was airlifted from one continent to another. That movement could never have been accomplished without a massive increase in our airlift capability, which is still being expanded. (It will have risen 400 per cent between 1961 and 1967). It required the development of new techniques to preposition combat equipment, of which we have two extra division sets now in Europe. It called for new techniques in military training and administration to make sure that units are really ready to move out on a moment's notice. This exercise, in which some 16,000 airmen and soldiers and more than 350 planes took part, is directly relevant to the needs of Europe, where it brought a seventh division to join the six that are to remain in place. It is also relevant to the ability of the U.S. to fulfill its policy commitments world-wide, swiftly and in effective strength.

But, it might be asked, what is the significance of all this for the realistic security problems of the United States and its allies? To what contingencies are these forces expected to contribute, and how effective might they be, measured against the strength of opposing forces? How meaningful is it to talk of sixteen or twenty or thirty divisions in opposing the ground armies of the Soviet Union and Communist China?

Such questions are often meant to be merely rhetorical, in view of the supposed masses of Communist troops. The fact is that they are serious, difficult questions, to which I shall suggest some tentative answers. But it is difficult to encourage realistic discussions of specific contingencies so long as the shadow of the Communist horde hangs unchallenged over the debate. The actual contingencies that seem to be to me most likely and most significant are not those which would involve all, or even a major part, of the Soviet Bloc or Chinese Communist armed forces, nor do they all involve Europe. Hence, aggregate figures of armed strength of NATO and the Warsaw Pact nations are not immediately relevant to them. But it is useful to make these over-all comparisons precisely because misleading or obsolete notions of these very aggregates often produce an attitude of hopelessness toward any attempt to prepare to meet Communist forces in ground combat, however limited in scope.

The announced total of Soviet armed forces for 1955 was indeed a formidable 5.75 million men. Today that figure has been cut to about 3.3 million; the Warsaw Pact total including the Soviets is only about 4.5 million. Against that, it is today the members of NATO whose active armed forces number over five million. The ground forces of NATO nations total 3.2 million, of which 2.2 million men are in Europe, as against the Soviet ground combat forces total of about 2 million men, and a Warsaw Pact total of about 3 million. Both the Soviet Union and the U.S. forces of course include units stationed in the Far East. In Central Europe, NATO has more men, and more combat troops, on the ground than does the Bloc. It has more men on the ground in West Germany than the Bloc does in East Germany. It has more and better tactical aircraft, and these planes on the average can carry twice the payload twice as far as the Soviet counterparts.

These facts are hard to reconcile with the familiar picture of the Russian Army as incomparably massive. The usual index cited to support that picture is numbers of total active divisions, and the specific number familiar from the past is 175 divisions in the Soviet Army.

This total, if true, would indeed present a paradox. The Soviet ground forces are reliably estimated to be very close to two million men, compared to about one million for the U.S. How is it that the Soviets can muster ten times the number of active, combat-ready, fully-manned divisions that the United States has manned, with only twice as many men on active duty? The answer is simply that they do not. Recent intensive investigation has shown that the number of active Soviet divisions that are maintained at manning levels anywhere close to combat readiness is less than half of the 160–175 figure.

What remains is a large number, but even that is misleading. For one thing, U.S. divisions have about twice as many men in the division unit and its immediate combat supporting units as comparable Soviet divisions. A U.S. mechanized division has far more personnel in maneuvering units, far more in armored cavalry, far more engineers, far more signals, far more light armored personnel carriers, and far more aircraft available in support than Soviet divisions. In addition to longer staying power, much of the U.S. manpower and equipment margin is muscle that would make itself felt on D-Day. If, on the other hand, we were to reorganize along Soviet lines, we could display far greater numbers of divisions comparable to those of the Soviets.

The Soviet combat-ready force remains a formidable one. Moreover, the Russians do have a powerful mobilization capability; in particular, they have a large number of lightly manned or cadre divisions to be filled out on mobilization. Still, this reality remains strikingly different from our accustomed maps of it.

I do not wish to suggest that such aggregate comparisons are by themselves a valid index to military capabilities. But they are enough to suggest the absurdity, as a picture of the prevailing military strengths on which new efforts might build, of David and Goliath notions borrowed from 1949.

None of this is to say that NATO strength on the ground in Europe is adequate to turn back without nuclear weapons an all-out surprise non-nuclear attack.

But that is not in any case the contingency toward which the recent and future improvements in the mobility and capabilities of U.S. general purpose forces are primarily oriented. Aggression on that scale would mean a war about the future of Europe and, as a consequence, the future of the U.S. and USSR. In the face of threats of that magnitude, our nuclear superiority remains highly relevant to deterrence. The Soviets know that even non-nuclear aggression at that high end of the spectrum of conflict so threatens our most vital interests that we and our allies are prepared to make whatever response may be required to defeat it, no matter how terrible the consequences for our own society.

The probability that the Soviet leaders would choose to invoke that exchange seems to me very low indeed. They know well what even the Chinese Communist leaders must recognize upon further reflection, that a nuclear war would mean destruction of everything they have built up for themselves during the last 50 years.

If we were to consider a spectrum of the possible cases of Communist aggression, then, ranging from harassment, covert aggression, and indirect challenge at one end of the scale to the massive invasion of Western Europe or a full scale nuclear strike against the West at the other end, it is clear that our nuclear superiority has been and should continue to be an effective deterrent to aggression at the high end of the spectrum. It is equally clear, on the other hand, that at the very low end of the spectrum a nuclear response may not be fully credible, and that nuclear power alone cannot be an effective deterrent at this level in the future any more than it has been in the past.

The fact is that at every level of force, the Alliance in general, and the U.S. Armed Forces in particular, have greater and more effective strength than we are in the habit of thinking we have—and with reasonable continued effort we can have whatever strength we need. I have spoken already of strategic weapons, where the great superiority of the United States is the superiority also of the Alliance. In tactical nuclear weapons a parallel superiority exists—and while many of our Allies share with us in manning the systems which would use these tactical warheads in the hour of need, it is not unfair to point out that, even more than in the strategic field, the tactical nuclear strength of the Alliance is a contribution of the United States. That strength has been increased, on the ground in Europe, by more than 60 per cent in the last two years. Today the thousands of U.S. warheads deployed on the continent for the immediate defense of Europe have a combined explosive strength more than 10,000 times the force of the nuclear weapons used to end the Second War. Tactical nuclear strength the Alliance has today, and we have provided it.

But neither we nor our Allies can find the detonation of such weapons—and their inevitable bilateral exchange—an easy first choice. At the lower end of the spectrum, therefore, we also need strong and ready conventional forces. We have done our part here and we continue to believe it just—and practicable—for our partners to do theirs.

The most difficult questions arise over the best means for meeting a variety of dangerous intermediate challenges in many parts of the world: those which threaten the possibility of sizable conflict while still not raising the immediate issue of the national survival of ourselves or of any member of our alliances. Conflicts might arise out of Soviet subversion and political aggression backed up by military measures in non-NATO areas in Europe, Latin America, the Middle East and Africa. There is a range of challenges that could arise from Communist China and its satellites in the Far East and in Southeast Asia. Most dangerously, approaching the upper end of the spectrum, there is the possibility of limited Soviet pressures on NATO territory itself, along the vast front running from Norway to Greece and Turkey. Both the flanks and the center contain potential targets. And always, of course, there are the contingencies that could arise in relation to Berlin.

It is difficult to say just how probable any of these circumstances might be, although they must be regarded as more likely than still larger aggressions. What one can say is that if any of these more likely contingencies should arise, they would be highly dangerous. Inaction, or weak action, could result in a serious setback, missed opportunity or even disaster. In fact, if either a nuclear exchange or a major Soviet attack should occur, it would most likely arise from a conflict on a lesser scale, which Western capabilities had failed to deter and which inadequate Western response had failed to curb in time.

Since World War II, the expansionist impulse of the Communist Bloc is clear, but equally clear is its desire to avoid direct confrontation with the military forces of the free world. In Greece, in Berlin, and in Cuba, Communists have probed for military and political weakness but when they have encountered resistance, they have held back. Not only Communist doctrine has counselled this caution, but respect for the danger that any sizable, overt conflict would lead to nuclear war. It would follow that no deterrent would be more effective against these lesser and intermediate levels of challenge than the assurance that such moves would certainly meet prompt, effective military response by the West. That response could confront the Soviets with frustration of their purposes unless they chose themselves to escalate the conflict to a nuclear exchange, or to levels that made nuclear war highly probable—a choice they are unlikely to make in the face of our destructive power.

The basis for that particular assurance cannot be systems in development, or weapons in storage depots, or reserves that must be mobilized, trained and equipped, or troops without transport. We need the right combination of forward deployment and highly mobile combat-ready ground, sea and air units, capable of prompt and effective commitment to actual combat, in short, the sort of capability we are increasingly building in our forces.

This capability requires of us—as of our Allies—a military establishment that is, in the President's words, lean and fit. We must stop and ask ourselves before deciding whether to add a new and complex weapon system to our inventory, whether it is really the most effective way to do the job under the rigorous conditions of combat. We must examine constantly the possibilities for combining functions, particularly in weapons that could be used by two or more Services. Given this tough-minded sense of reality about the requirements of combat readiness, it should be possible for the United States not only to maintain but to expand this increased strength without overall increases in our defense budget. As our national productivity and our gross national product expand, the defense budget therefore need not keep pace. Indeed, it appears likely that measured in relative— and perhaps even absolute—terms, the defense budget will level off and perhaps decline a little. At the same time, we are continuing the essential effort to reduce the impact of Defense spending on our balance of payments. We have already brought this figure down from $2.7 billion in fiscal year 1961 to $1.7 billion for fiscal year 1963, and we shall continue to reduce it, without reducing the combat ground forces deployed in Europe, and while strengthening our overall combat effectiveness.

And it must be our policy to continue to strengthen our combat effectiveness. I do not regard the present Communist leaders as wholly reckless in action. But recent experience, in Cuba and, on a lesser scale, in Berlin, has not persuaded me that I can predict with confidence the sorts of challenges that Communist leaders will come to think prudent and profitable. If they were again to miscalculate as dangerously as they did a year ago, it would be essential to confront them, wherever that might be, with the full consequences of their action: the certainty of meeting immediate, appropriate, and fully effective military action.

All of our strengths, including our strategic and tactical nuclear forces, contributed last year, and they would contribute in similar future situations to the effectiveness of our response, by providing a basis for assurance that the Soviets would not dangerously escalate or shift the locale of the conflict. But above all, in order to fashion that response, and to promise the Soviets local defeat in case of actual ground conflict, we had to use every element of the improvements in combat readiness and mobility that had been building over the preceding year and a half, including combat divisions, air transport, and tactical air. And the last ingredient was also there: the will to use those forces against Soviet troops and equipment.

Let us not delude ourselves with obsolete images into believing that our nuclear strength, great as it is, solves all of our problems of national security, or that we lack the strengths to meet those problems that it does not solve. In the contingencies that really threaten—the sort that have occurred and will occur again—we and our allies need no longer choose to live with the sense or the reality of inferiority to the Soviet Bloc in relevant, effective force. Let us be fully aware of the wide range of our military resources, and the freedom they can give us to pursue the peaceful objectives of the free world without fear of military aggression.

Leo Szilard: THE MINIMAL DETERRENT

One of the physicists contributing to the development of the first atomic bomb, Leo Szilard subsequently devoted his efforts to controlling the use of the bomb and preventing war. In this article he explores the possibility that as few as forty H-bombs, out of the existing American arsenal of tens of thousands, would be enough to deter the Soviet Union from a strategic nuclear attack. In doing so, he directly criticizes Mc-Namara's "damage-limiting strategy."

WE are close to the point where America and Russia could destroy each other to any degree and, therefore, one would perhaps think that the arms race is about to come to an end. In fact, a new arms race might be just around the corner.

Russia might before long deploy antimissile-missiles in defense of her rocket-launching sites. For such a defense to be effective it is only necessary to prevent a ground burst of the incoming rockets and this is, quite possibly, an attainable goal. Thus, the administration might find itself under congressional pressure to double, or triple, the number of Minutemen scheduled to be built in order to overcome Russia's defense of her bases.

Russia might go further and might deploy antimissile-missiles also for the defense of some of her larger cities. If she does, we would be forced to do likewise. There is this difference however: Russia could deploy antimissile-missles around a few of her largest cities and stop there, but if we deployed antimissile-missiles around any of our cities, the administration would be under pressure to deploy such missiles around every one of our cities.

Because fallout could kill most people in a city if Russia were to explode suitably constructed bombs at some distance from the city, it would make little sense for us to deploy antimissile-missiles around our cities without also embarking on a program of building fallout shelters for the protection of the population of these cities.

Economic considerations might slow Russia's build-up of her antimissile defenses sufficiently to make it still possible for us to avoid such a new arms race by reaching an agreement with Russia on a cut-off in the production of bombs and rockets.

Russia would perhaps agree to such a cut-off—as a first step—if America and Russia were to reach a meeting of the minds on reducing their strategic striking forces, step by step, to a level *just sufficient* to inflict "unacceptable" damage in a counterblow in case of a strategic strike directed against their territory.

An agreement providing for a reduction of America's and Russia's strategic striking forces to such a "minimal" level would also have to provide for adequate measures of inspection. It would take very stringent measures of inspection indeed to make sure that no bombs and rockets whatever remain hidden in Russia, but as long as we retain a striking force large enough to inflict unacceptable damage on Russia in a counterblow, we could be satisfied with rather limited measures of inspection. In this case, we would need to have just enough inspection to make sure that Russia would not secretly retain a strategic striking force large enough to be capable of destroying a significant portion of the "minimal" striking forces which we retain. The same considerations also hold true, of course, in the reverse for Russia.

Many of those who joined the Kennedy administration in 1961 have come to believe that we would be much more secure in the years to come if we concluded with Russia an agreement based on the concept of the minimal deterrent. In the course of the last year, Russia has accepted the notion that America as well as Russia may retain a small strategic striking force until the "end of the third stage" of the "disarmament agreement," and that inspection shall not be limited to equipment which is to be destroyed, but be extended also to equipment which is being retained.

We shall have to explore whether the Russians mean the same thing as we do when they appear to accept the principle of the "minimal deterrent." We shall be able to discover this, however, only if we first find out what we mean ourselves when we speak of this principle.

We may as well start out by asking ourselves how large the strategic forces retained would need to be in order to fulfill their function.

If Russia retained twelve rockets and bombs of one to three megatons each which could reach their target, then Russia's counterblow could demolish twelve of our largest cities totaling over 25 million inhabitants. Clearly, this would be

unacceptable damage, since in none of the conflicts which may be expected to arise in the foreseeable future would we be willing to pay such a price for the sake of attaining the political objectives involved.

Because Russia has fewer large cities, we might have to retain about forty bombs if our retaliatory counterblow is to demolish Russian cities housing over 25 million people.

Both America and Russia could maximize their immunity to undetected violations of the agreement by maintaining a certain balance between landbased long-range rockets and submarine-based rockets, within the limitations set by the agreement.

The warheads carried by antimissile-missiles may have to be limited to perhaps twenty kilotons each and to a total of, say, three megatons for Russia and for America alike. The deployment of antimissile-missiles around cities may have to be prohibited.

It is my contention that we need to reduce the strategic striking forces down to the level of the "minimal deterrent" as soon as possible, because of the perils we face when we reach the end of the current transitional period.

Had a conflict between Russia and America led to an armed clash a few years ago and had, at some point along the line of escalation, Russian made a sudden attack against America's strategic air bases and rocket bases, then America's "residual striking capacity" would have been sufficient to demolish, in a counterblow, all of Russia's sizable cities. But if, conversely, America had made such an attack against Russia's air bases and rocket bases of *known location*, Russia's residual counterblow could not have caused any comparable destruction.

Today, America's strategic atomic

striking forces are presumably still superior to those of Russia, by a factor of perhaps between three and ten, in the number of hydrogen bombs that they could deliver and, presumably, America could maintain this kind of numerical superiority in the years to come. She could not, however, by doing so, keep Russia from steadily increasing her "residual striking capacity." In recent years, Russia has steadily proceeded with the hardening of her rocket-launching sites and the building of additional submarines capable of launching long-range rockets. Today, she has reached the point where her "residual counterblow" would be sufficient to demolish most of America's major cities on the eastern seaboard and some of her cities in the west. This is a higher price than America would be willing to pay for reaching her political objectives in any of the conflicts that might be expected to occur in the predictable future. In other words, today Russia's "residual striking capacity" would be sufficient to inflict "unacceptable damage" on America. Conversely, America's residual striking capacity would be sufficient today to *demolish all of Russia's cities of over 100,000.*

It might be true that today America would still be able to recover from an all-out atomic war, whereas Russia would lose all of her cities of over 100,-000 and thus suffer a destruction of her society from which she would not recover.

In the situation in which we find ourselves at present we no longer try to "deter" Russia with threatening a massive strategic strike against her cities. We realize that today such a threat would come very close to being a threat of murder and suicide, and clearly a threat of this sort would not be believable in any conflict in which major Amer-ican interests might be at stake, but not America's existence as a nation. Instead, we are currently maintaining a military posture which threatens to lead step by step to an escalation of the war and ultimately to our accepting "unacceptable" damage, in return for the virtually complete destruction of Russia's society. We maintain this military posture in order to discourage Russia from embarking on any military conquest.

Right after the Second World War, the security of Western Europe was threatened by the combination of communist pressure from the inside and the possibility of a Russian military intervention from the outside. Today, the Russians would be exceedingly unlikely to embark on a conquest of Western Europe whether or not we maintained our current military posture, but—because of the military posture we maintain—if a war broke out, as the result of a border incident or an uprising in Eastern Germany, it would be likely to escalate and to end up with an exchange of strategic atomic strikes between America and Russia.

Presumably only conventional weapons would be used at the outset of such a war. At some point during the see-saw of fighting, Russia might be tempted, however, to send her troops in hot pursuit across the prewar boundary, and they might penetrate deep into Western territory. In case of a deep penetration of Western Europe by Russian troops, our plans call for the use of tactical weapons, not only in combat against troops which have penetrated the prewar boundary, but also against the lines of communications of the Russians in Eastern Germany, Poland, and Russia herself. If, conversely, certain NATO units were to penetrate into Eastern Germany, the Russians would presumably bomb communication lines in Western Europe, including the ports where American troops disembark. Because the size of tactical bombs ranges all the way from one kiloton to several hundred kilotons, there is no substantial gap between where tactical bombings end and where strategic bombings begin. Thus, a war that neither America nor Russia wanted could easily end up in an all-out atomic war between them.

The risk that such a war in Europe might end up in an all-out atomic war is the price we are paying for maintaining our present military posture. To my mind this is far too high a price to pay for deterring Russia from something that she wouldn't be likely to do anyway.

A meaningful agreement on arms control based on the concept of the minimal deterrent would limit not only the number of the strategic bombs retained, but also the number, as well as the size, of the tactical bombs retained. The size of these bombs might be limited to one kiloton and America, as well as Russia, might each be limited to perhaps 300 such bombs.

The total tonnage of the tactical bombs retained by either side would thus amount to only a few per cent of the total tonnage of the strategic bombs retained by them but still it would amount to about ten per cent of the tonnage of high explosives dropped during the last world war.

By establishing a wide gap between the size of the tactical bombs retained, one kiloton, and the size of the strategic bombs retained, presumably about one megaton or larger, one may establish a clear distinction between bombs which might be used against troops in combat and bombs which have been retained only to be used in a counterblow, in retaliation for a strategic strike.

America ought to resolve and to proclaim that she will not resort to the use of tactical bombs if there is a war in Europe, except in case of a 100-mile-deep penetration of Western Europe by Russian troops and would then use them only within the Western side of the prewar boundary—as long as Russia imposes similar limitations upon herself. Then, if a war were to start in Europe which neither America nor Russia wanted, it would be less likely to end up with an exchange of strategic strikes between America and Russia.

Even the limited numbers of tactical bombs retained could have an important effect on the course of the war, if such a war were to break out in Europe, and their effect could be to slow down the war and stabilize a front across Europe, provided that America and Russia imposed upon themselves the restraints spelled out above. For if Russian troops were to cross in hot pursuit the prewar boundary and were to penetrate one hundred miles deep into Western Europe, with America in possession of tactical bombs the Russians could not very well mass troops and conventional armor at any point in front of the American defense line in sufficient strength to break through that line. Conversely, Russia would gain the same advantage from her possession of tactical bombs if certain NATO units were to cross the prewar boundary and were to penetrate one hundred miles deep into Eastern Europe. The fear that atomic bombs might be dropped on troops massed for a breakthrough would thus tend to stabilize a front across Europe, giving time for tempers to cool and for ending the war by a settlement. However, no agreement providing for arms control would be likely to withstand the strain of a *protracted* war in Europe.

SATURATION PARITY

In the last few years, Russia has steadily proceeded with the building of submarines capable of launching rockets and with the hardening of her long-range rocket bases, located on Russian territory. It is clear that, in time, Russia must reach the point where her "residual striking capacity," would be large enough to demolish all of America's sizable cities. *At that point Russia will have achieved parity of saturation.* Russia may reach saturation parity, at a modest economic sacrifice, within a very few years.

General LeMay said, in a major speech (reported in the *Washington Post* of December 18, 1963), that those who argue that the United States has an extensive overkill, favor cutting American strategic striking forces so they would only be capable of hitting cities. He said that such a reduced force would leave the United States too weak "to destroy the enemy's nuclear forces before they destroy us," and that America's maintenance of "superior counterforce strength" gives American policymakers the widest range of credible options for controlled responses to aggression at any level. According to General LeMay, this paid off during the Berlin and Cuban crises in which the United States forced Russia to back down, and won her political objectives because the Russians knew that the United States had a clear margin of strategic nuclear strength.

I do not propose to take issue with General LeMay at this point, except to say that the "deterrent effect" of America's margin of strategic nuclear strength obviously comes to an end when the striking forces of the Soviet Union reach saturation parity with those of the United States. If our "margin" was in fact responsible for Russia's yielding in the Berlin and Cuban crises, then if another similar crisis were to occur, after Russia reaches saturation parity, we would no longer have any reason to expect that Russia would yield always.

Had Russia not yielded in the Cuban crisis of October 1962, and had her ships continued on their course to Cuba in defiance of America's proclamation of a partial naval blockade of that island, American warships would have sunk Russian ships. No one can say how far escalation would have gone and whether Russia, being unable to resist America in the Caribbean, would have retaliated elsewhere, perhaps in Europe.

General LeMay believes that, if it had come to an armed clash in the Cuban crisis, the Russians would have put an end to escalation at some point along the line. But even if one were to accept this view, one could still not predict which of the two countries would take the first step to halt escalation if a similar clash were to occur a few years hence in the symmetrical situation of saturation parity. And, if it is no longer possible to say who would put an end to escalation, then also one cannot predict just how far escalation might go. In saturation parity, escalation might go to the point where all of America's and all of Russia's cities of over 100,000 get demolished.

Manifestly, saturation parity presents a threat to the survival of our society.

Let us now consider how saturation parity may be expected to affect our allies in general and Western Germany in particular.

Let us ask ourselves, for example, what would have happened if there had occurred a few years ago a major uprising in Eastern Germany against the established government and if substantial units of armed West German volunteers had moved into East Germany to assist the insurgents. Presumably, at first one would not have known with certainty whether these volunteers were acting with the tacit approval and active participation of the West German government, or whether they were acting against its wishes and in disregard of its orders. Had such a contingency occurred a few years ago, the odds are that America would have extended protection to West Germany against the strategic striking forces of Russia, on the ground that America must prevent the destruction of West German military power. America would have been likely to extend such protection to West Germany whether Germany was or was not the aggressor, and if there had been any doubt on this score, Germany would have been given the benefit of the doubt.

If a contingency of this sort were to occur in the years to come, and if the Russians were to fear that the clash might escalate into an all-out atomic war, they might decide to knock West Germany out of the war by dropping, all at once, between five and ten hydrogen bombs on West German cities. Having done this, Russia would then be in position to speak to America as follows: "German aggression forced us to do what we did, lest the clash of arms escalate into an all-out atomic war, which neither Russia nor America wants. We realize that America could now respond by demolishing one Russian city after another, but for every Russian city that America may demolish, Russia would demolish one American city. Let's be rational about this. What has happened, has happened; let's see now where we go from here. Russia does not intend to occupy any West German territory and she is willing to put up a few per cent of

her industrial output to help rebuild the cities of West Germany, provided her contribution is matched, dollar-for-dollar, by America."

The Russians would hardly assume that the Americans would respond in a rational fashion if they were to drop bombs on American cities but, in the contingency described above, they might, rightly or wrongly, expect a rational response if they demolished German cities only and refrained from extending their attack to America's own territory.

The nations of Europe are becoming gradually aware of the situation they will face in saturation parity and they are beginning to ask themselves whether each may not have to maintain a strategic striking force under its own control in order to safeguard its own security.

Few people contemplate with equanimity the possibility that Germany may acquire a substantial atomic striking force. There are those in America who believe that we might keep Germany from wanting to have such a striking force under her own control by setting up a strategic striking force under the joint control of America and Germany, with perhaps a few other nations joining in. The multilateral strategic striking force under discussion would be equipped with two hundred Polaris missiles, enough to demolish two hundred cities if all of them were to reach their target, yet it would not give the Germans what they need in saturation parity as long as America can veto the use of this force. There is reason to believe that the Germans propose to participate in it only because they assume that it may be possible for them to get rid of the veto.

The creation of such a strategic striking force would make it possible to endow West Germany, by the mere stroke of a pen, with a striking force of her own, a force corresponding in size perhaps to the financial stake that Germany would have in the joint force. Those Americans who advocate the setting up of such a joint force in order to keep the Germans from having a force under their own control follow the principle of the lesser evil. Following this same principle could lead to transferring to Germany control of a part of the joint force later on if the Germans should proclaim that they would otherwise build a substantial striking force of their own.

It is doubtful whether control over atomic bombs can be kept from the Germans by a gadget like the multilateral nuclear striking force, or for that matter by any gadget, *and it is probably true that in the long run it would be impossible to prevent the proliferation of atomic bombs if saturation parity were to prevail.*

Under an agreement based on the concept of the "minimal deterrent" which would leave Russia in possession of, say, twelve bombs and rockets, Russia would put herself at a disadvantage if, in the contingency discussed above, she were to use up five to ten of her twelve bombs and rockets in a "first strike" against German cities. If she were to do this, she would have only two to seven bombs and rockets left in comparison to the forty bombs and rockets retained by America, and she would therefore put herself at a disadvantage in the crisis that would follow her attack. In this sense, an agreement limiting Russia to twelve bombs and rockets would provide protection to the cities of our allies in Western Europe, but this would be true only if we could be certain that Russia would not secretly retain, say, another twelve strategic bombs and rockets which are operational or

could be made operational on short notice. The measures of inspection instituted at the outset of the agreement would not be likely to give any certainty in this regard, because initially we might have to be satisfied with measures of inspection which give us assurance that *Russia cannot secretly retain a striking force large enough to be capable of destroying a significant fraction of our minimal striking forces.*

It is therefore necessary to explore what additional measures of inspection would provide our allies with the protection they need, and whether such measures would be acceptable to Russia.

In an extended conversation I had with Chairman Khrushchev in October of 1960, I said that, even if Russia were willing to admit international inspectors in unlimited numbers, it would not be possible for us to be sure that there would not remain a few bombs and rockets hidden somewhere in Russia which are operational or could be made operational very quickly. I told Khrushchev that I believed that the Soviet government could reassure the world in this regard only if they were to create conditions in which we could rely on a Soviet citizen reporting secret violations of the agreement to an international authority. He got the point, got it fully, and his answer was very gratifying.

I would not attach as much significance to this as I do if I had not accidentally discovered in December of the same year, when I attended the Pugwash meeting in Moscow, that some of our colleagues of the Soviet Academy of Sciences scheduled to attend this meeting had been given a detailed report of my conversation with Chairman Khrushchev. In this report, Khrushchev was quoted to have said to me that, for the sake of making general disarmament acceptable to the United States, the Soviet government would give serious consideration to creating conditions which would make it possible for the world to rely on a Soviet citizen reporting violations of the disarmament agreement to an international authority.

After the Pugwash meeting, I stayed on in Moscow for about a month and had numerous private conversations with our Russian colleagues. I wanted to discover, most of all, whether the Soviet government could, if it wanted to, create conditions in which the world could rely on Russian citizens reporting violations of the disarmament agreement. I finally concluded that this would not be easy but that it would be done, provided the arms control agreement offered Russia a substantial increase in her security and permitted the Soviet government to divert substantial funds from armament to other uses.

I believe that it would be much easier to get the Soviet government to accept very far-reaching measures of inspection for the sake of obtaining an objective that makes sense to them than to get them to accept quite limited measures of inspection for the sake of any "first steps" which would not offer any major direct benefits to Russia.

Speaking before the Economic Club of New York on November 18, 1963, Secretary McNamara stated that we have now more than 500 operational long-range ballistic missiles and are planning to increase their number to over 1,700 by 1966. In addition, we have today over 500 bombers on quick-reaction ground alert. In his speech, McNamara refers to the "damage-limiting capability of our numerically superior forces," which I take to mean our capability of making massive attacks against

Russia's strategic air bases and rocket bases.

It is my contention that we will not be able to negotiate a meaningful agreement on arms control until we are willing to give up what General LeMay calls our "capability to destroy the enemy's forces before they destroy us," and that by giving it up we would gain more than we would lose.

If I were given an opportunity to cross-examine General LeMay, I would ask him what contingencies he has in mind when he speaks of "destroying the enemy's nuclear forces before they destroy us." It would then turn out that, while we could invoke the "damage-finding capability of our numerically superior forces" by making a massive attack against Russia's strategic air fields and rocket-launching sites of known location in certain conceivable contingencies, these contingencies are very contrived and most unlikely to occur.

The "damage-limiting capability of our numerically superior forces" might have a certain marginal value in the least probable contingencies, but in the most probable contingency, if a war were to break out which neither Russia nor America wanted, then our capability of making a sudden massive attack against Russia's rocket-launching sites of known location would render an escalation of the war more likely than less likely. For if the superiority of our strategic striking forces is anywhere as great as General LeMay claims, the Russians might fear at some point that our next move in the pursuit of war would be the waging of a massive strike against their rocket bases of known location, and at that point they might be driven to launch rockets against our cities and the cities of our allies from all of their bases that are vulnerable to an attack.

There is no need to belabor this point, however, because the "superiority of our strategic striking forces" of which General LeMay speaks is at best a vanishing asset. Within a few years, we shall have saturation parity, and in that situation Russia will no longer have to fear a massive strike against her rocket bases of known location.

In saturation parity—as far as the strategic striking forces are concerned—America and Russia will find themselves in a fully symmetrical situation, and at this time the only meaningful choice before us is between the symmetrical situation of saturation parity, in which both America and Russia maintain strategic striking forces at a high level, and another symmetrical situation in which they both maintain strategic striking forces at a "minimal level."

More and more people within the administration realize that it would be futile and increasingly dangerous to continue to use our strategic striking forces as a deterrent the way we used them in the past, and that *these forces must be used only for the purpose of threatening a counterblow in case of an atomic attack directed against our territory.* Those who take this position inevitably arrive in time at realizing that both America and Russia would gain, rather than lose, in security by reducing their strategic striking forces from the level of saturation parity to the level of the minimal deterrent.

We must ask ourselves at this point under what conditions would Russia want to have an agreement based on this concept, and want it strongly enough to be prepared to pay the price in terms of the measures of inspection needed.

I think that Russia would have no desire to enter into such an agreement unless she could be sure that it would not be necessary for her later on to abrogate the agreement and to rebuild her atomic striking forces, so to speak, from scratch. Thus, Russia would have to be convinced that Germany is not going to have under her own control an atomic striking force, and also that China would not build a substantial atomic striking force of her own.

I do not know what it would take to induce China to forego having atomic bombs, but it is conceivable that China might be willing to go along with an agreement on arms control that would leave America and Russia in possession of minimal strategic striking forces, provided that in return America would agree not to resort to the use of either strategic or tactical atomic bombs in the Far East and Southeast Asia, and to set up an atom-free zone that would include these areas.

There are those who say that America could not agree to forego the use of atomic bombs in the Pacific because it might be necessary to use atomic bombs in the defense of Formosa.

Quite similar views were voiced at the Disarmament Conference of the League of Nations which was held in Geneva in the 1930s. At issue at this conference was the elimination of the bomber plane from the national arsenals and the outlawing of bombing from the air. At one point during the negotiations, Anthony Eden, who was at that time a civil servant, told the conference that His Majesty's government could not be a party to the outlawing of bombing from the air. He said that, from time to time, the Royal Air Force engaged in bombing the mud huts of the unruly tribes of the northern frontier of India and that this was the only effective way to keep these tribes from making periodic incursions into Indian territory. Some people have no sense of proportion.

It is probably true that we cannot have general disarmament without also having a far-reaching political settlement. The conclusion of an agreement providing for arms control based on the concept of the minimal deterrent need not, however, await a political settlement in Europe or elsewhere. Moreover, in view of our current estimates of Russia's military manpower and resources, we need no longer insist that the reduction of the number of bombs and rockets to a minimal level must be accompanied by the reduction of the conventionally-armed forces. Rather, we may rely on economic considerations to limit the armies maintained by the nations of Europe, including Russia.

The reduction of the strategic striking forces to the "minimal" level spelled out above need not take place at the very outset of the agreement, all at once, but there would have to be substantial step-by-step reductions to intermediate levels soon after the agreement goes into force. What matters is not so much in what steps and just how fast a reduction of the strategic striking force takes place, but rather whether America and Russia are in full agreement on the level of the "minimal" striking forces which would be retained under the agreement.

In these circumstances, Russia and America could enter into conversations aimed at reaching a meeting of the minds on the reduction of the number of atomic bombs and rockets to a minimal level and could thereafter seek the concurrence of the other nations, including Germany and China.

If these conversations were carried far enough to convince the Russians that an agreement could be negotiated without running into any major hitches, then the Russians might accept a production cut-off in bombs and rockets even before an agreement based on the minimal deterrent is fully spelled out with the i's dotted and the t's crossed, and for the purposes of a production cut-off the United States would presumably be satisfied with inspection limited to production facilities of known locations.

POSTSCRIPT

I do not know anyone in the Department of Defense who would not on the whole agree with the analysis, given above, of the perils of saturation parity and the security to be gained from the "minimal deterrent." Some people in the Defense Department might say that I am overstating my case, that it would not be sufficient for us to retain forty large bombs and rockets because only a certain fraction of the Polaris and Minutemen launched would reach their target, the rest being duds. They might say therefore that, instead of forty bombs and rockets, we ought to retain perhaps 100 or 150 of them. These are not essential differences because, as the reliability rating of our rockets increases, their numbers could be more or less automatically reduced.

Others in the Defense Department might say, not publicly but privately, that I am understating my case when I say that Russia may achieve saturation parity within a few years, and that Russia has achieved saturation parity already. This is not an essential difference either.

I should perhaps add that I am not personally acquainted with any of those in the Defense Department who are part of the "military-industrial complex" of which President Eisenhower spoke in his presidential farewell address, and who have a vested interest, emotional or otherwise, in maintaining large strategic striking forces. Even though these people do not occupy top positions in the administration, they must be reckoned with because they have considerable influence in Congress.

While the "military-industrial complex" might well attempt to block any significant reduction of our strategic striking forces, when such a reduction becomes a "clear and present danger" our current failure to make any decisive progress on arms control must not be attributed to them. Rather, this failure is mainly due to our method of negotiating with the Russians.

We have not made, thus far, and are not likely to make in the predictable future, a formal proposal on arms control which the Russians could accept as it stands, for fear that the proposal would become the starting point of "horse trading" and that we would end up with an agreement that might endanger our security.

Each time we introduce a new feature into our proposals which we hope could create a basis for negotiations, it takes the Russians about six months to respond. This sluggishness of the Russian response is not surprising because there are few people concerned with the problem of arms control working within the Russian government who are capable of coping with the unprecedented problems involved. These few men have their hands full taking care of the day-to-day problems and cannot devote much time to long-term planning. This may well be

the reason why the Russians take so long to respond, even if we propose something that clearly would be in their interest to accept.

The number of those working within our administration who can cope with these problems is larger, but it is not large. These men are plagued by being uncertain as to what the Russians would be likely to accept and also what Congress would be likely to accept.

What the Russians would accept and what Congress would accept depends on whether the administration can make them understand the need to avoid a new arms race, the perils which we face in the current situation, and the advantages that an agreement based on the concept of the minimal deterrent would hold for all concerned. Unless it becomes somehow possible to arrange for greatly improved communication between the administration and the Soviet government, on the one hand, and between the administration and Congress, on the other hand, no decisive progress toward a meaningful agreement on arms control is going to be made. Instead, we might be taking a number of little steps, like the test ban, for instance. These little steps improve the international climate, but if nothing decisive is done before long, the climate may keep on improving and improving until there is a new crisis, and then we shall be back where we started from. To make progress is not enough, for if the progress is not fast enough, something is going to overtake us.

John F. Kennedy: A TRUCE TO TERROR

This article presents the major part of an address delivered by President Kennedy before the United Nations General Assembly in September 1961. He renews on behalf of his administration the commitment of the Eisenhower administration that the United States would seek "general and complete disarmament under effective international control." The commitment did not affect immediate military expenditures (indeed, the defense budget rose by $10 billion during the first year of the Kennedy administration), but a symbolic step toward the achievement of disarmament was taken by the Kennedy administration in 1963 with the conclusion of a treaty banning nuclear tests.

TODAY every inhabitant of this planet must contemplate the day when this planet may no longer be habitable. Every man, woman, and child lives under a nuclear sword of Damocles, hanging by the slenderest of threads, capable of being cut at any moment by accident or miscalculation or by madness. The weapons of war must be abolished before they abolish us.

Men no longer debate whether armaments are a symptom or a cause of tension. The mere existence of modern weapons—ten million times more powerful than anything the world has ever seen and only minutes away from any target on earth—is a source of horror and discord and distrust. Men no longer maintain that disarmament must await the settlement of all disputes, for disarmament must be a part of any permanent settlement. And men may no longer pretend that the quest for disarmament is a sign of weakness, for in a spiraling arms race a nation's security may well be shrinking even as its arms increase.

For 15 years this Organization has sought the reduction and destruction of arms. Now that goal is no longer a dream; it is a practical matter of life or death. The risks inherent in disarmament pale in comparison to the risks inherent in an unlimited arms race.

It is in this spirit that the recent Belgrade conference, recognizing that this is no longer a Soviet problem or an American problem but a human problem, endorsed a program of "general, complete and strictly and internationally controlled disarmament." It is in this same spirit that we in the United States have labored this year, with a new urgency and with a new, now-statutory agency fully endorsed by the Congress, to find an approach to disarmament which would be so far-reaching yet realistic, so mutually balanced and beneficial, that it could be accepted by every nation. And it is in this spirit that we have presented, with the agreement of the Soviet Union, under the label both nations now accept of "general and complete disarmament," a new statement of newly agreed principles for negotiation.

But we are well aware that all issues

From President John F. Kennedy, "Let Us Call a Truce to Terror." Address before the U.N. General Assembly, September 25, 1961.

of principle are not settled and that principles alone are not enough. It is therefore our intention to challenge the Soviet Union, not to an arms race but to a peace race—to advance together step by step, stage by stage, until general and complete disarmament has been achieved. We invite them now to go beyond agreement in principle to reach agreement on actual plans.

The program to be presented to this assembly for general and complete disarmament under effective international control moves to bridge the gap between those who insist on a gradual approach and those who talk only of the final and total achievement. It would create machinery to keep the peace as it destroys the machines of war. It would proceed through balanced and safeguarded stages designed to give no state a military advantage over another. It would place the final responsibility for verification and control where it belongs—not with the big powers alone, not with one's adversary or one's self, but in an international organization within the framework of the United Nations. It would assure that indispensable condition of disarmament—true inspection—and apply it in stages proportionate to the stage of disarmament. It would cover delivery systems as well as weapons. It would ultimately halt their production as well as their testing, their transfer as well as their possession. It would achieve, under the eye of an international disarmament organization, a steady reduction in forces, both nuclear and conventional, until it has abolished all armies and all weapons except those needed for internal order and a new United Nations Peace Force. And it starts that process now, today, even as the talks begin.

In short, general and complete disarmament must no longer be a slogan, used to resist the first steps. It is no longer to be a goal without means of achieving it, without means of verifying its progress, without means of keeping the peace. It is now a realistic plan and a test—a test of those only willing to talk and a test of those willing to act.

Such a plan would not bring a world free from conflict or greed, but it would bring a world free from the terrors of mass destruction. It would not usher in the era of the super state, but it would usher in an era in which no state could annihilate or be annihilated by another.

In 1946, this nation proposed the Baruch plan to internationalize the atom before other nations even possessed the bomb or demilitarized their troops. We proposed with our allies the disarmament plan of 1951 while still at war in Korea. And we make our proposals today, while building up our defenses over Berlin, not because we are inconsistent or insincere or intimidated but because we know the rights of free men will prevail—because, while we are compelled against our will to rearm, we look confidently beyond Berlin to the kind of disarmed world we all prefer.

I therefore propose, on the basis of this plan, that disarmament negotiations resume promptly and continue without interruption until an entire program for general and complete disarmament has not only been agreed but has been actually achieved.

PROPOSALS TO HALT TESTING AND NUCLEAR ARMS RACE

The logical place to begin is a treaty assuring the end of nuclear tests of all kinds, in every environment, under workable controls. The United States and the United Kingdom have proposed such a treaty that is both reasonable, effective, and ready for signature. We are still prepared to sign that treaty today.

We also proposed a mutual ban on atmospheric testing, without inspection or controls, in order to save the human race from the poison of radioactive fallout. We regret that that offer was not accepted.

For 15 years we have sought to make the atom an instrument of peaceful growth rather than of war. But for 15 years our concessions have been matched by obstruction, our patience by intransigence. And the pleas of mankind for peace have met with disregard.

Finally, as the explosions of others beclouded the skies, my country was left with no alternative but to act in the interests of its own and the free world's security. We cannot endanger that security by refraining from testing while others improve their arsenals. Nor can we endanger it by another long, uninspected ban on testing. For 3 years we accepted those risks in our open society while seeking agreement on inspection. But this year, while we were negotiating in good faith in Geneva, others were secretly preparing new experiments in destruction.

Our tests are not polluting the atmosphere. Our deterrent weapons are guarded against accidental explosion or use. Our doctors and scientists stand ready to help any nation measure and meet the hazards to health which inevitably result from the tests in the atmosphere.

But to halt the spread of these terrible weapons, to halt the contamination of the air, to halt the spiraling nuclear arms race, we remain ready to seek new avenues of agreement. Our new disarmament program thus includes the following proposals:

First, signing the test ban treaty by all nations. This can be done now. Test ban negotiations need not and should not await general disarmament.

Second, stopping the production of fissionable materials for use in weapons and preventing their transfer to any nation now lacking in nuclear weapons.

Third, prohibiting the transfer of control over nuclear weapons to states that do not own them.

Fourth, keeping nuclear weapons from seeding new battlegrounds in outer space.

Fifth, gradually destroying existing nuclear weapons and converting their materials to peaceful uses; and

Finally, halting the unlimited testing and production of strategic nuclear delivery vehicles and gradually destroying them as well.

WORLDWIDE LAW AND LAW ENFORCEMENT

To destroy arms, however, is not enough. We must create even as we destroy—creating worldwide law and law enforcement as we outlaw worldwide war and weapons. In the world we seek, the United Nations emergency forces which have been hastily assembled, uncertainly supplied, and inadequately financed will never be enough.

Therefore, the United States recommends that all member nations earmark special peacekeeping units in their armed forces, to be on call of the United Nations, to be specially trained and quickly available, and with advance provision for financial and logistic support.

In addition, the American delegation will suggest a series of steps to improve the United Nations' machinery for the peaceful settlement of disputes, for on-the-spot factfinding, mediation, and adjudication, for extending the rule of international law. For peace is not solely a matter of military or technical problems; it is primarily a problem of politics and people. And unless man can match his strides in weaponry and technology with equal strides in social and political development, our great strength, like that of the dinosaur, will become incapable of proper control and, like the dinosaur, vanish from the earth. . . .

Barry M. Goldwater: WHY NOT VICTORY?

In 1962, Barry M. Goldwater, then senator from Arizona, vehemently disagreed with the Kennedy position on disarmament in a book called Why Not Victory? *He argued that recent official foreign policy was disastrous for American interests and liberty. This position appealed to many conservatives and became a factor in helping Goldwater win the Republican Presidential nomination in 1964. Here Goldwater explains why the United States ought not to adopt a policy of world disarmament.*

THE idea of disarmament is a beautiful one. No man can deny that. In practical realistic terms, however, at this moment in history, the disarmament concept is an effective weapon in the hands of the Communists and a danger to the freedom of mankind.

I suppose that ever since man has resorted to armaments other than his fists, he has dreamed about and talked about each side throwing down its weapons so that the danger of conflict would be banished forever. Now if the disagreements and misunderstandings that make armaments necessary could be discovered and removed, then we could discuss removing the arms. But as long as people have a basic loyalty to their own country's aims and policies and their own way of life, those people will be necessarily concerned with the retention of those things and will fight for them with any and all weapons they can put their hands on.

If I might use the old "tail wags dog" analogy, this basic understanding between people is the dog and disarmament is the tail that must follow. But right now the proponents of disarmament, years ahead of themselves, are making the tail wag the dog.

I don't propose to go back through the history of the failure of these disarmament proposals. Rather I will confine myself to discussing some obvious reasons why they will not work in the world today as they have not worked in the world of yesterday. The reasons never change. In doing this, I hope that we can recognize the advantage which has accrued to the Soviet thus far in these phony disarmament talks. It is another lesson that will serve us well as we proceed in the winning of this Communist War.

Often, in speaking about the current efforts of Khrushchev to entice us into tricky disarmament discussions, I have likened Russia to a giant of a man, maybe six feet ten inches tall, weighing 275 pounds, trim and hard as nails, who with one swipe of his hand could render me "hors de combat." But this giant never bothered me because I had in my possession a pistol which he knew I would use as an "equalizer" if he made one threatening move toward me. This worked fine but one day he turned to me and said, "Goldwater, let's you and I talk disarmament."

Now who would be expected to do the disarming? I would, of course; and the moment I yielded to this silly demand, I would be at his mercy. Put Russia in the giant's place and the Western Powers in mine and the hypothetical situation—though a crude one, I admit—begins to make a little sense. Russia with her land mass and her large and well-equipped ground and sea forces has been held in check by our "equalizer," which is overwhelming air power and the nuclear bomb. What would be the subject of disarmament talks? Why, air power to be sure, because ground and sea power are historical in their dimensions and we just do not discuss traditional weapons in such meetings. And the moment we began to yield on air power, we would be placing ourselves in a position of irreparable weakness. . . .

When we begin to talk seriously of world-wide disarmament and the procedures, the mechanics, the methods of accomplishing it, the path becomes a maze no man or country could follow without great difficulty. Most thinking people agree at the outset that total disarmament can never be achieved because of the need inside each country for enough weapons to maintain local order and control lawless elements. So it becomes, even at the start, a question of *partial* disarmament. And here further compli-

cations set in. If, for instance, the decision were reached to halve the world's armaments, how would we develop an arrangement that was equitable all around? We cannot assume that we would all start from the same position. Some are stronger than others and some are pitifully weak. Halving would leave the strong strong when compared to the weak, who would only be made weaker. But let us bypass this problem. In this hypothetical case of halving, how would we go about it? Would we abolish bombers but retain fighter craft because in the case of local revolution they could be useful? (Fighters also carry most kinds of bombs and rockets.) Would we abolish the submarine and retain light carriers? (Planes from light carriers can drop bombs.) Would we abolish the warhead but retain the bomb? (Bombs can have important peacetime uses, such as the creation of harbors.)

If, on the other hand, the approach were to allow each country to retain weapons in ratio to its population, we would be faced with the ridiculous situation of China and India in a mad arms race to catch up with their population —while the highly developed countries of the West would be throwing their arms away.

Now suppose that the nations of the world, sitting around a conference table, agreed to eliminate the atomic and nuclear bombs altogether for wartime use as weapons but approved of the fission process for peaceful uses. Two problems would face us. The country having the largest number of soldiers (Russia or Red China) would have the largest inventory of conventional weapons, so we in the West would be at an immediate disadvantage. The second problem is the old one of inspection: who will see to it that some peacefully intended use of the fission process is not clandestinely turned into a monstrous weapon to be used just once to begin and end a war?

Now the mere fact of the existence of nuclear weapons does not make disarmament an imperative policy. I do not subscribe to the theory that nuclear weapons have changed everything—that we must now have complete disarmament or the world will go up in flames. And even if I did subscribe to such a theory, how would I or anyone else ever be assured that our enemy in the Communist War would adopt a similar attitude? Certainly, the Russians will not adopt any kind of disarmament so long as revolt lies seething just below the surface in their satellite nations. We have in the nuclear bomb an advance in weaponry, and terrible though that advance is, it still is merely a more efficient means of destruction. In a historical and relative sense, it can be compared with the advance made in military operations by the invention and adaption of gunpowder to war-making and the development of aerial warfare and strategic bombing missions.

The only real disarmament will come when the cause for arms is removed. In our case that cause is communism. In the Soviets' case, that cause is the free world. Does anyone believe that they will voluntarily give up their gains and their objectives? Does anyone believe that we will give up our way of life and settle for peace under slavery? Those few among us who, because of a paralyzing fear of death itself, would rather be "red than dead" need a lesson in history. The idea of freedom cannot be stamped out by the scratch of a pen. Patrick Henry said it in a few ringing words two hundred years ago, and his "Give me liberty or give me death" rings just as true today.

On the other side of the coin, the ideas of power and control of people and their lives are not going to be discarded easily by the rulers of communism, to be traded for the ideologies of free men. Especially is this true because Communists have, with the use of relatively few weapons, gained control over one-third of the people of this earth and already foresee the day when universal and complete success will be theirs. Ideas are what we are talking about, and ideas are not materially destroyed as we would destroy a piece of paper or a car or a house. They are replaced by other ideas—sometimes by better ideas and sometimes by worse. Our job is to prove and sell our set of ideas—not to destroy by disarmament the means we have of protecting them if that becomes necessary.

History teaches us that armament races are no more than a symptom of international friction, not a cause of it. Unless the basic disagreement between the Western world and communism can be resolved, any suggestion of disarmament is illusory and deceptive.

The Communists are dedicated to the destruction of the Western world, by peaceful means if possible, by war if necessary. We cannot by dropping our guard, by diminishing our ability to defend ourselves, create a situation conducive to world peace. In fact, it is probable that any disarmament by the Western world would be construed by the Russians as a sign of weakness and an invitation to a Communist thrust.

The Communist leaders may preach general disarmament for propaganda purposes. They may also seriously promote mutual disarmament in certain weapon categories in the knowledge that their superior strength in other weapons would leave them, on balance, decisively stronger than the West. Thus, in the light of the West's comparative weakness in conventional weapons, it might make sense for the Communists to seek disarmament in the nuclear field. If all nuclear weapons suddenly ceased to exist, much of the world would immediately be laid open to conquest by the masses of Russian and Chinese men under conventional arms.

We should, I believe, announce in no uncertain terms that we are *against* disarmament. We are against it because we *need* our armaments—all of those we presently have, and more. We need weapons for both the limited and the unlimited war. . . .

Charles E. Osgood: RECIPROCAL INITIATIVE

Charles E. Osgood, an experimental psychologist at the University of Illinois and one-time president of the American Psychological Association, tried to bring to bear on world affairs the research done by psychologists on hostility and conflict among individuals and small groups. Osgood here proposes a strategy for achieving disarmament by reducing conflict one step at a time, recommending that the United States begin independently to use this strategy as a way of forcing the Soviet Union to follow suit. This article by Osgood became one of the most important intellectual roots of the political demands of such peace groups as the National Committee for a Sane Nuclear Policy. It also became a prime example to many scholars of one way of making their own particular scholarly interests relevant to "peace research."

M OST Americans are filled with the basically irrational conviction that the only way to avoid military conflict with the Communist world is to prepare for it. . . . Unconsciously projecting our own norms and values, we feel threatened when they are not adhered to and attribute it to the essential boorishness and deceit of others. By encouraging self-delusion and condoning a double standard of national morality, our psycho-logic has created an oversimplified world inhabited by angels and bogy men. Everything becomes channeled into this one overwhelming polarity of good and evil. . . . Faced apparently with such powerful and expanding evil, mounting anxiety narrows our perspective, robs us of our problem-solving capacity, and forces us into the most stereotyped and traditional responses to external danger—maintaining a threatening posture and building weapons as fast as we can. Now *if* the enemy is in truth inhuman and completely unlike us, then we have no choice but to kill and be killed. Or, if the enemy is entirely human and much like us, *but* we and he continue to hew inflexibly to present policies, then nuclear holocaust is equally inevitable.

Nuclear deterrence has frozen initiative in foreign policy along traditional lines. Paradoxically, the very capacity for destruction which nuclear technology represents, the very power it confers, serves to inhibit freedom of action by those who possess it. Is there any solution? Can't we get rid of these new weapons and go back to the almost friendly pattern of "war as usual"? No, we can never go back—the scientific knowledge that yields the nuclear technology is irreversible. Can't we somehow reach mutual agreements with the Russians on disarmament? The prospects are not good, as we have seen. The same forces that have created the arms race militate against success in mutual negotiations—and it is not only the Russians with whom we must negotiate. Unilateral acts of an aggressive, tension-*increasing* nature have become prohibitively dangerous, and therefore the whole notion of power politics has now become anachronistic. We stand with terrible power but shorn of initiative. What about unilateral acts of a tension-*reducing* nature? Abject unilateral disarmament is unfeasible; it asks American Man to act in a uniquely civilized way and to assume that Russian Man would respond in kind—but human culture is not ready for such a big step. However, there are other forms of unilateral, tension-reducing action, and these we must now explore in the hope of discovering some way out of the Great Freeze.

The Arms Race in Reverse

Imagine two husky men standing facing each other near the middle, but on opposite sides, of a long and rigid seesaw balanced over an abyss. As either man takes a step outward, the other must compensate with a nearly equal step outward on his side or the balance will be destroyed. The farther out they move, the greater the unbalancing effect of each step, and the more agile and quick to react both men must become to maintain the precarious equilibrium. To make the situation even worse, both of these husky men realize that this teetering board has some limit to its tensile strength—at some point it is certain to crack, dropping them both to destruction. So both men are frightened, but neither is willing to admit it for fear the other might take advantage of him.

How are these two men to escape from this dangerous situation, a situation in which the fate of each is bound up with that of the other? One reasonable solution immediately presents itself: Let them agree to walk slowly and carefully back toward the center of the teetering board in unison. To do this they must trust each other. But these men do not trust each other, and each supposes the other to be irrational enough to destroy them both unless he (Ego) preserves the balance. But now let us suppose that it occurs to one of these men that perhaps the other is just as frightened as he is and would also welcome some way of escaping from this intolerable situation. So this man decides to gamble on his new insight and calls out loudly, "I am taking a small step *toward* you!" The other man, rather than have the precarious balance upset, also takes a tentative step forward, whereupon the first takes yet another, larger step. Thus they work their ways back to safety by a series of unilateral, yet reciprocal, steps—very much as they had originally moved out against each other.

As a form of international behavior, the arms race is a case of graduated, but reciprocal, unilateral action. It is obviously unilateral, in that the nation developing a new weapon, increasing its stockpile, or setting up a new military base does not make its action contingent upon any agreement with the other side. It is reciprocal because each increment in military power by one side provides the stimulus for intensified efforts by the other to catch up and get ahead. The arms race is necessarily graduated: first, by the irregular and somewhat unpredictable pace at which scientific technology develops and second by oscillating national moods of fear and relative complacency. Is it possible that the arms race provides a model for its own reversal? Graduated and reciprocated unilateral action of a tension-*reducing* nature is certainly conceivable—but is it feasible under present conditions? In the remainder of this paper I will try to show that, given the same dedication and effort we have been pouring into the arms race, its reversal is certainly feasible; more than that, given existing capacities for nuclear retaliation, some policy of this sort may well be the only avenue left for positive foreign policy.

Graduated Reciprocation in Tension Reduction

Perhaps the most general characterization of my proposal would be that it asks for a deliberate "peace offensive" designed to induce reciprocation by an enemy. It is an offensive in deeds rather than words, but the deeds are carefully graduated in magnitude of risk so as to maintain tolerable levels of dignity and security. The actions we might undertake would be highly diversified and an opponent would not be able to predict their time and place, but all our actions would be intended to reduce tensions. The range of acts envisaged is much broader than "disarmament" and even broader than "disengagement," as usually conceived, since much more than arms control is involved, and even "engagement" in certain cooperative activities would be included. The goal is reversal of the tensions/arms-race spiral and creation of an atmosphere in which steps toward a more permanent solution of the problem of survival in the nuclear age can be taken. The following principles are intended to guide us to this goal.

Inducing Reciprocation

1) *Our unilateral acts must be perceived by an opponent as reducing his external threat.* To be most effective in inducing an opponent to reciprocate, the initiator must attempt to reduce his opponent's level of tension so that the opponent, in turn, acquires increased freedom for action. This means that the acts must not be advantageous to the initiator in terms of military aggression; they may or may not be militarily disadvantageous—although, of course, militarily disadvantageous actions have an additional degree of "bonafideness." As we shall see later in a hypothetical example, the ways in which perception of external threat may be reduced are many and varied.

2) *Our unilateral acts must be accompanied by explicit invitations to reciprocation.* In the recent history of Russo-American relations there have been many instances of unilateral, tension-reducing actions on both sides, but they have been largely abortive—because they were not announced in advance as part of a consistent policy, were not explicit as to expected reciprocation, and were

therefore never disentangled from the cold war. It is the fact that reciprocation is expected which must be made explicit. Reciprocation might be the same or different in kind, depending on the nature of the initiating act and it need not be objectively balanced in quantity; as Fisher has pointed out, the burden of an identical rule may be quite different in two countries (e.g., openness of inspection in the United States and the U.S.S.R.). In some cases the invitation to reciprocation may be entirely open-ended, leaving the selection of appropriate response up to the opponent, or we may merely intimate what we hope for in return for our concession. Explicit invitation to reciprocate serves several purposes: it encourages the opponent actively to consider tension-reducing alternatives; it assures him that we will correctly interpret his action; and it indicates that we believe his motives parallel, if not identical, to ours.

3) *Unilateral acts must be executed regardless of prior commitment by the opponent to reciprocate.* This is the characteristic that distinguishes this policy most clearly from mutual negotiation and allows a reasonable degree of initiative. We have already seen how attempts at negotiating agreements under conditions of high tension are bedeviled by biased perceptions of what is equable and by self-fulfilling prophecies. As long as we remain chained to the requirement of prior commitment by the opponent, our freedom of action is greatly restricted, as is his. Furthermore, our execution of a previously announced action serves to contradict cries of "cold-war propaganda," and the opponent's prophecy is *not* fulfilled—which is a significant learning experience for him. Furthermore, as Fisher has also pointed out, unilateral action has distinct advan-

tages where perceptions of what is equable are biased or where the same rule might be unequally burdensome on two countries—it is more flexible in that it allows for equality of intent and spirit despite inequality in specific performance.

4) *Unilateral acts must be planned in sequences and continued over considerable periods regardless of reciprocation by an opponent.* Where the announcement of an initial act may be greeted with cries of "propaganda" by an opponent, particularly since it would be small in magnitude of risk, and where even its subsequent execution could still be considered a cold-war "trick," the announcement and then execution of the next—and the next, and the next—makes it harder and harder to maintain this interpretation. Not only is the self-fulfilling prophecy being repeatedly denied, but the bogy-man conception of their enemy (ourselves) is becoming less tenable—the machinations of psycho-logic (ordinarily reinforced by the threatening posture of the enemy) must become more and more complex and ludicrous until they fall of their own weight. This, again, is a forced learning process we are able to induce unilaterally. Maintaining a series of unilateral, tension-reducing acts produces a cumulative pressure toward reciprocation.

5) *Unilateral acts must be announced in advance of execution and widely publicized to ally, neutral, and enemy countries as part of a consistent policy.* Tension-reducing acts are likely to lose some of their impact if announcement and execution are coincident. Rather, time intervals between announcement and execution should be planned, these being just sufficient for rational consideration by an opponent, for his preparation of reciprocative action, and for world opin-

ion to mobilize. This means that the time interval will necessarily vary with the nature of the act. However, the announcement of each act should include the proposed time of execution; otherwise, both the announcement and the execution would lose much of their force. General public announcement should be made for several reasons: first, many of our acts would invite reciprocation from several or even all other countries; second, one of the major pressures toward reciprocation by the opponent would come from favorable reactions in the neutral or uncommitted nations; third, we would be interested in offering a new model of international behavior to all nations. Linking each announced action with a consistent policy of tension reduction through graduated and (hopefully) reciprocated unilateral acts would serve both to disentangle it from the cold war and to augment its cumulative impact by explicit identification with other actions, past and future.

Maintaining Security

1) *Unilateral acts must be graduated in risk potential, should they not be reciprocated or should they be exploited by an opponent.* Being a highly unconventional international policy, because of both its unilateral and its non-aggressive nature, graduated and reciprocated tension reduction is liable to suspicion abroad and resistance at home. Therefore, its initial phases must be viewed as a learning experience on both sides of the fence. If the correct national behavior is to be acquired, the probabilities of reward must be considerably higher than the probabilities of punishment. In general, earlier unilateral acts would be smaller in magnitude of risk than later acts. Furthermore, the initial series of acts would be so designed as to maxi-

mize the likelihood of clear reciprocation being obtained (e.g., involve issues where we know the opponent is eager to move positively) and minimize the likelihood of resistance at home (e.g., involve issues where security seems to be less concerned than general human welfare). Whatever scoffing there might be at the insignificance of our initial acts would be resolved in the continuation of the program. Another basis for graduation throughout would be whether or not reciprocation for previous acts had been obtained; failure would be followed by acts of lower risk potential and success by acts of higher risk potential. This stresses the need for extraordinary intelligence, information, and flexibility in the design and maintenance of such a policy—which should be viewed as a challenge rather than a flaw.

2) *Unilateral acts must be diverse in nature and unpredictable (by an opponent) as to locus of application and timing in series.* The only thing that binds together the separate actions envisaged in this policy is their tension-reducing impact upon an opponent (and, indirectly, upon ourselves). Their nature and area of application can and should be diverse. This is in order that reduction of tension and pressure toward reciprocation on the opponent can be maintained cumulatively without progressively weakening ourselves in any one area. Thus, an act in one area (e.g., inviting diplomatic exchange with Communist China) would be followed by a number of acts in quite different areas (e.g., on controls and inspection vis-à-vis Russia, on joint provision of technicians for the Congo, etc.) before we would return to another step in the China area again. The locus of application and timing of our unilateral acts must be unpredictable by the opponent to prevent his usur-

pation prior to our announcement of intention. I submit that the likelihood of an opponent taking an aggressive initiative (e.g., Communist China invading the islands of Quemoy and Matsu), and his support by world opinion if he does, is much less if we have already announced that we intend to take the relevant action as of a certain date.

3) *Unilateral acts must never endanger our "heartland" or reduce our fundamental capacity for retaliatory second strike.* I take it for granted that in the very near future both Russia and the United States will have ready an effective second-strike nuclear force, whether consisting of "hardened" land bases or of mobile, nuclear-powered submarines armed with Polaris-type missiles, or both. This is an awesome fact of life which may have redeeming features; it may offer the psychological support for tension-reducing actions within tolerable limits of security—*provided that* (a) the retaliatory, second-strike nature of this power is continually emphasized and (b) the minimum power necessary for effective deterrence, rather than an arms race, is maintained. This minimum capacity for effective deterrence should not be reduced by unilateral action (even though other forms of armament could be), but rather its elimination should be arrived at through negotiation, in the atmosphere of greater confidence and trust produced by the policy we are discussing. The reason for preserving our retaliatory capacity while continuing a program of tension reduction is that it is this capacity for near annihilation on both sides that both encourages reciprocation and prevents overstepping. The reason for not initiating actions which might endanger our "heartland" is again that, if taken advantage of, we would be likely to release full-scale retaliation and

thereby write "finis" to this chapter of the human book. This proposal for "nuclear deterrents last" is novel and quite the opposite of most disarmament proposals, which ask for "nuclear disarmament first and popguns last." I firmly believe I am right in this—as long as nationalistic tensions and technical know-how exist, popguns can start conflicts that end in nuclear devastation.

4) *Unilateral acts of tension-reducing nature must be accompanied by explicit firmness in all areas.* This may sound like a bit of fine sophistry, but it is no more so than the way a wise parent encourages spontaneity in his child in prescribed situations but without letting down the bars all over the house. In the present case this means that announcements of unilateral actions would be accompanied by explicit warning that encroachment in this or any other area would be resisted firmly. Indeed, should such encroachment occur—and one can be certain that under present conditions of nuclear deterrence it would be partial, tentative, and probing—we would have to deal with it firmly, just as if the policy of tension reduction were not in effect. Here yet again we would have a kind of learning experience for any opponent as well as ourselves—learning that unilateral action does not mean "softness" or "surrender." However, just as the wise parent does not take away all privileges from his child and forever lock him in the cellar for a single misdemeanor, so the action we would take for a specific encroachment should be pinpointed to that event in both word and deed, i.e., designed to restore the *status quo*. And once the *status quo* was restored, the program of graduated tension reduction should continue as before, without reprisals. It is apparent that this policy represents something

quite different than the traditional "Neanderthal" conception of international relations; maintaining the initiative would require both firmness of purpose and exercise of self-restraint, by the government, by the military, by the mass media, and ultimately by the public at large—but the stakes are high and the policy is appropriate to the nuclear age. . . .

A Hypothetical Program

The following hypothetical program of unilateral actions assumes several broad areas of application. (A. Science and Secrecy; B. Communist China; C. Controls and Inspection; D. Socioeconomic; E. Military) and several levels of risk potential or significance (1, 2, . . . N) within each area. It is assumed that the periods of various actions (between announcement and execution) may overlap and that an opponent may or may not reciprocate in any particular instance. It is also assumed that our announced actions are executed on schedule.

April 1: We announce that, as of May 1, we intend to make public all medical information we have been gathering concerning man in space; reciprocation invited from all nations; nature of general policy indicated (A1).

May 1: We announce that, as of May 15, all discriminatory trade and travel restrictions with respect to Communist China will be lifted, and we will entertain diplomatic exchange; reciprocation in kind is invited and general policy stated (B1).

(A1 reciprocated by Russia and most other countries.)

May 20: We announce a unilateral test ban that will be continued indefinitely and invite reciprocal announcement from Russia, England, and France (C1); we also announce that we are

making technicians and professionals in various fields of specialization available to the UN for work in the Congo and other areas; reciprocation from other "have" nations invited and general policy again stressed (D1).

(B1 not reciprocated by Communist China.)

June 1: We announce that at the next convening of the General Assembly of the UN (June 20) we will move the seating of Communist China; we again indicate our willingness to entertain diplomatic exchange and the general nature of our policy (B2).

(C1 reciprocated by Russia, England, and France; D1 reciprocated by England, France, and others, but not Russia.)

June 15: We announce that, as of July 15, one of our overseas bases in Japan will be publicly denuclearized, and we invite UN and Russian inspection; reciprocation is invited but left open-ended, and our general policy is again stressed (E2).

(On June 16 bombardment of Quemoy and Matsu increases abruptly and invasion preparations are observed; U.S. naval power concentrates and firm warnings about what our policy does and does not imply are given; Russia makes nuclear threat; on June 20 we nevertheless move seating of China in UN; one invasion attempt is repulsed [but no counterattack on Chinese mainland occurs]; Russo-Chinese conferences are followed by Chinese delegation seated in UN; Quemoy-Matsu hostilities peter out; D1 reciprocated by Russia.)

August 1: We announce that, as of next September, student exchanges will be offered in proportion to the populations of the countries involved; reciprocation is invited generally (A2). We announce that, as of August 20, the DEW Line (early warning system) will be made bidirectional (warning of our flights toward Russia as well as vice versa), and we invite the Soviets to "plug in" (NOTE: I am told this is technically feasible; it emphasizes our reliance on second-strike rather than first-strike strategy; if we have no intention of surprise attack, there is no reason why this shouldn't be done); reciprocation in kind invited (C2).

(Russia announces that, as of September 1, its armed forces in East Germany will be reduced by one third and reciprocation in form of denuclearization of West Germany invited; we interpret this as indirect reciprocation of E2; an envoy from Peking arrives in Washington for talks.)

August 15: We announce that, with agreements from some of the major mass media, beginning September 1, material on contemporary world affairs prepared by Russian sources may appear on Sundays in special newspaper sections and certain TV and radio programs without censure; reciprocation in kind invited (D2).

(We announce that, as of September 1, NATO forces are being reduced in West Germany but that no denuclearizing is contemplated at this time; East Germany announces relaxation of transit regulations between West Germany and West Berlin; B1 reciprocated by Communist China.)

September 1: We announce that, as of January 1, we will be prepared to have all launchings of flights into outer space supervised by a new agency of the UN which we propose be established (A3).

(Russia announces an expanded program of inviting scholars and scientists for advanced study in Soviet institutes [which we interpret as indirect reciprocation for A2]; Communist China invites joint teams of Russian and American scientists to Peking for conferences on technical problems; C2 and D2 still not reciprocated by Russia.)

September 15: We announce that, as of October 15, the islands of Quemoy and Matsu will be publicly demilitarized and turned over to proper authorities from the mainland, and clear statements about the unchanged status of Taiwan are made (B3); we announce that surpluses of several grain crops will be made available at adjusted prices to countries needing them during the winter (D3); reciprocations left open-ended.

(Russia proposes that, beginning January 1, the conquest of space be made a joint human enterprise on the model of the International Geophysical Year [IGY] and invites international cooperation through the UN [we interpret this as reciprocation for A3]; C2 and D2 still not reciprocated by Russia; Nehru urges that she do so.)

November 20: We announce that, as of the next meeting of the UN (December 1), we will move the substitution of Communist China for Nationalist China on the Security Council—reciprocation in the form of recognition of Taiwan as a sovereign country with representation in the General Assembly requested (B4); we announce that, as of February 1, we will open this country unilaterally to inspection and monitoring by authorized UN teams, as further evidence that we have no intention of surprise attack—reciprocation in kind is invited from all countries (C4).

(The demilitarization and evacuation of Quemoy and Matsu accomplished without major incident [Chiang Kai-shek's threats of retaliation countered by large non-military spending program in Taiwan]; Russia has reciprocated, in part, on C2, but not D2; under strong urging from Great Britain, plans for full-scale disarmament negotiations under UN auspices are being prepared.)

Does this read like something out of *Fantasy and Science Fiction?* It certainly must in detail. It is presented as a purely hypothetical sequence of events—I have no crystal ball! The time scale is obviously compressed for convenience, and the many difficult and worrisome details of communication and counter-communication, misunderstanding and clarification, probing and holding off are necessarily short-circuited. However, a number of probable characteristics of the process are illustrated. For one thing, it is apparent that much of the reciprocation obtained would be made to appear as initiation by the opponent, inviting our reciprocation. This is obviously desirable, as long as the unilateral initiations are in the right direction, but it means that we must be flexible and quick-witted in estimating the nature and magnitude of such steps and in preparing our own reciprocations. For another thing, it is suggested that differences in the perception of what is equable would often mean that their reciprocations would seem inadequate but their requests exorbitant (and vice versa, of course). However, one of the advantages of unilateral and reciprocated action is that agreements on what is equable are not required—each side merely monitors its own subsequent unilateral action in terms of its perception of prior reciprocation.

Assumptions Underlying This Policy

Graduated reciprocation in tension reduction is based on the assumption that the problems we face are essentially matters of human nature and human relationships, and therefore that solutions must be found in how human beings think and how their judgments, attitudes, and beliefs can be influenced. It assumes that the Russian people and leaders are more like us than like the bogy men our psycho-logic creates, and that they are as eager to reduce the chances of full-scale nuclear conflict as we are. It assumes that the men in the Kremlin are susceptible to pressures, both from within and from without, since such pressures are an index of the success or failure of their system; and particularly it assumes that the less dogmatic Communists, like Khrushchev, are concerned about the mounting pressures from China. It assumes that the Communists are as convinced that their way of life will win out in non-military competition for men's minds as we are (or should be) that ours will. And finally, therefore, it assumes that the Russians would accept an unambiguous opportunity to reduce world tensions for reasons of good sense *even* if not for reasons of good will. . . .

Some Likely Objections to This Policy

There are many deep-seated objections to any unilateral, non-aggressive policy of this sort, and it will be well to anticipate them. I have had the benefit of critical discussions of this proposal with colleagues in many fields, and I think they have helped press it into clearer form. Objections tend to fall into two general classes: those based on more emotional grounds and those based on more rational or practical grounds.

The most deep-seated objection to the policy I have outlined stems from what I have called the bogy-man conception of the enemy. Many people will argue that any unilateral act designed to reduce tensions would be interpreted by the Russians as a sign of weakness and, given their despotic drive toward world communism, would encourage them to encroach further on the free world. I cannot deny this as a possibility, even though I consider it remote. But, if this is their inherent nature, then we should make sure of it before the present balance of power has shifted to any significant degree. At least we would have made a sincere effort to test their intentions, and the risk involved should be more than offset by a gain in favorable world opinion. Surely it would be a tragedy, a cause of cosmic irony, if two of the most civilized nations on earth were to drive each other to their mutual destruction because of their mutually threatening conceptions of each other —without ever having tested the validity of these conceptions.

Some Americans will see this policy as a deliberate subversion, a Communist-inspired Trojan horse. My argument that it is actually a strategy designed to get us out of a serious dilemma, and in the long run to preserve our way of life, would be incomprehensible to them. Psycho-logic lubricates the groove along which we slide those who disagree with us into the Communist camp—particularly when the disagreement involves matters of basic security. However, everything that isn't blue doesn't have to be red, and similarly everyone who disagrees with our present policy doesn't have to be following the Communist line. The fact that this objection flows more from emotion than from reason does not minimize its effectiveness.

Many more people will probably see this policy as the coward's way. They would interpret it as a proposal that we surrender without a fight, a kind of "moral disarmament," and therefore entirely distasteful. For Americans, pacifism may be weak but good in time of peace, but in time of war ("cold" or "hot") it easily becomes weak and bad. This, too, is as illogical a criticism as it is potent. The man who relies on his brain rather than his brawn is not necessarily a coward—particularly when his brawn is peculiarly susceptible to the effects of radiation. And, in any case, it can hardly be called "surrender" if the unilateral acts designed to reduce tensions are made deliberately, on our own initiative, and as a means of applying pressure on an opponent to reciprocate.

Probably many people, however, will see this policy as an idealist's fantasy—certainly not one that faces up to the hard realities of the world we live in. They would say that to weaken one's own position in any way in the present situation is as softheaded as it is softhearted. However, what seems realistic within one's time-bound frame of reference may be highly unrealistic in the broader scheme of things. As I pointed out in an earlier section, what we call "realistic" usually depends upon what is habitual, what is familiar, and upon immediate goals. Thus it is "realistic" to concentrate on earning a living, getting one's children through school, and getting a little fun out of life, but it is "idealistic" to concentrate upon the world of the future. So, too, is it deemed realistic to demand more weapons when faced with external threat and idealistic to worry about where it is all leading. But novel situations demand new definitions of what is realistic, and now we are certainly in a novel situation. The real idealists today, as Marc Raskin put it to me so well, are those who actually believe that the arms race can be continued indefinitely without something going wrong, who actually believe that the men behind the nuclear weapons are suprarational and will behave like so many computers.

More rational objections to this policy might come from those who agree with the logic of my general argument but nevertheless come to the conclusion that it is simply not feasible under present conditions. And they would probably be referring not so much to Russian reactions as to our ability to initiate such a policy here at home. Existing public attitudes, coupled with my own principle of psycho-logic they would say, make it likely that even if such a policy were adopted and sponsored by thoughtful and courageous leaders, both it and they would be rejected by the vast majority of people in this country. My answer is that unpopular causes have been won before. It is not easy, and today it would require equal courage and dedication on the part of those who determine policy in the mass media. But attitudes and beliefs can be changed. During the period when Russia became our ally and defended Stalingrad, some of my own research at the time showed that we came not only to think of Russians as much more *kind, noble,* and *fair,* but even as more *Christian!* And this happened in the brief span of a few months. Changes in public attitudes and beliefs depend particularly on events—if not those that occur inadvertently in the world, then those that are produced by men whose opinions count.

What about the objection that even graduated unilateral action involves too much risk? Although this policy does involve risk—indeed, the open and explicit assumption of risk is essential for its acceptance by an opponent—I believe that such risk must be taken in the interest of our long-term security. Our present policies, as I have tried to show, involve equal or even greater risk, but yet offer little hope in the long run of either preserving our way of life or guaranteeing our physical security. We must simply accept the fact that *there is no policy, no alternative we can choose, that entails no risk.* The best we can do is to weigh the risks involved in different policies against the ultimate security that might be achieved.

Another objection on the grounds of feasibility has been this: Is it possible to have acts that reduce tensions to any significant degree that do not at the same time endanger our heartland? In the first place I would argue that there is no perfect correlation between the military significance of events and their psychological impact, and this policy is concerned with maintaining psychological pressure. The Russians' first sputnik and their more recent shot at the moon did little to change the balance of military power, but they certainly had far-reaching psychological effects on the people of the United States. Recognition of Communist China on our own initiative likewise would have psychological impact far beyond its military significance. In devising programs of unilateral action it would be necessary to consider most carefully what does and what does not constitute actual military potential. Furthermore, the real "defense" of our heartland under present conditions lies only in deterrence, in our second-strike capacity. And here, as Milburn has argued so cogently, I think, there is a certain minimum capacity for retaliation that has a near maximum deterrent effect upon an opponent—to be able to annihilate him ten or a hundred times over probably doesn't deter him much more than to be able to annihilate him just once! Properly appreciated, this fact should free us both economically and intellectually for more rational endeavors than the arms race.

This leads to another criticism—that this policy seems to amount to betrayal of our obligation to defend our allies. Although it is true that graduated reciprocation in tension reduction would mean reducing our military support in some areas where communism is in delicate balance with more liberal political views, does this necessarily imply defeat of our way of life in these areas—particularly if we were to succeed in reducing tensions between East and West generally? In the long run, the so-called "underdeveloped" countries will achieve greater security if we and the Russians stop using them as pawns in a global chess game. Most importantly, our own security in a nuclear age is coming to depend less and less upon allies or upon territorial control—particularly as intercontinental missiles with nuclear warheads become available. Just as we would not now risk starting a full-scale war for some remote foreign objective, so is our own liability to attack coming to be independent of geographic distance. The British are already well aware of this sobering fact, as evidenced by the Labour party's position on unilateral disarmament. And even if we were, against our own self-interest, to engage in continuous "brushfire wars" about the perimeter of the free world, one can reasonably ask in just what sense this "defends" other nations. In the sparring of the two giants, it is the little countries on whose soils the skirmishes take place who suffer the most severe wounds. . . .

Finally, there are some questions of practicality. Even assuming we were to undertake such a policy, would the Russians accept our unilateral acts and we their reciprocations, as bona fide? Applying the same arguments I brought to bear against achieving mutual agreements through negotiation under conditions of stress, wouldn't the Russians perceive our acts as cold-war deceptions? And wouldn't we be even more distrustful of their apparent reciprocations without any hard and fast agreements about inspection and the like? I would argue, first, that our real protection against being "tricked" or "taken advantage of" lies in our undiminished capacity for second-strike retaliation, and exactly the same thing is true for the opponent. Second, and perhaps most important, unilateral acts, unlike mutual discussions, have the status of *fait accompli,* just like the satellites circling our globe. It is difficult to deny the fact of their commission (particularly if they are announced in advance and can be publicly observed), and argument over the motivation of the first tends to be resolved by execution of the second. Third, not only would it be difficult for the Russians to practice deception over the long run but we have good reason to believe (cf. arguments under "assumptions" above) that they are as eager to ease tensions as we are. Finally, as to our distrust of Russian reciprocations, there is a principle of human behavior that is relevant here: Man A's interpretation of Man B's reaction to him depends heavily upon A's own prior behavior toward B. If American Man has already made an intentional conciliatory act toward Russian Man, he is much more likely to perceive the Russian's reciprocation as bona fide than if it came unsolicited.

But what if one side tried to take advantage of the other's unilateral actions? Wouldn't this have the "boomerang effect" of even further intensifying mutual bogy-man conceptions? Here would be the self-fulfilling prophecy with a vengeance! This, of course, is the risk we take, but with graduated unilateral action the initial risks are small. Actually, I think the real danger would not lie so much in deliberate encroachments by either side on the other as in failures to appraise correctly the risks and benefits in particular unilateral acts or reciprocations as seen by the other side. Thus what might be perceived by the Soviets as a big concession in the area of inspection, we might consider piddling—and once again we are back in the problem of biased perceptions of the equable. As Fisher has put it, "unless there is a good deal of negotiation and communication between the two sides they will not know what is bothering each other, what steps each side thinks it can undertake, and what steps it considers equivalent." This obviously puts a premium on preparation of our policy makers in depth and breadth; it also means that such a policy should be accompanied by a high level of informal communication designed to modulate the reciprocative acts. In practice, the graduated and unilateral characteristics of the process should provide ample room for mutual adjustments.

I believe that, even granting the atmosphere of mutual distrust in which such a process must be begun, both internal and external pressures of public opinion would force the opponents into at least token reciprocations at the low-risk level at which this policy would be initiated. And here another principle of human behavior becomes relevant: when people are made to keep on behaving in ways that are inconsistent with their actual attitudes (e.g., as if they really trusted each other), their attitudes tend to shift into line with their behavior. In other words, I think that if we could initiate a series of reciprocated, tension-reducing acts and maintain them over a sufficiently long period, the basic attitudinal conditions that now prevent us from taking larger, more significant steps toward world peace would be eliminated. . . .

Robert Strausz-Hupé:

THE DISARMAMENT DELUSION

One strategist who vigorously disagreed with proposals for disarmament was Robert Strausz-Hupé, director of the Foreign Policy Research Institute at the University of Pennsylvania. Here he argues that an examination of Soviet history shows that calls for disarmament have been means of emotionally disarming the West; and that an examination of present Soviet interests demonstrates that world disarmament would benefit the Soviets more than the West.

ON September 18, Premier Khrushchev, whom we have learned to address as "Mister Chairman," presented to the General Assembly of the United Nations a program for general and complete disarmament. He prefaced the proposal with a ringing appeal to peace: "So long as there exist large armies, air forces, and navies, nuclear and rocket weapons, so long as young men on the threshold of life are first of all taught to wage war while the general staffs work out plans for future military operations, there is no guarantee of stable peace."

Mr. Khrushchev proposed nothing less than that "over a period of four years, all States should effect complete disarmament and should no longer have any means of waging war." Armies, navies, and air forces should "cease to exist." General Staffs and War Ministries are to be abolished, military educational establishments closed, military bases on foreign soil dismantled. All atomic and hydrogen bombs will be destroyed, and their further production terminated. Missiles of all ranges will be liquidated. "At the disposal of States there should remain only strictly limited contingents of police (militia) agreed for each country, armed with small arms and intended exclusively to maintain internal order and protect the personal security of citizens."

Khrushchev's bland offer obviously caught U. S. officials off guard. After hours of silence, State Department spokesmen and several leaders of the Senate stated that the proposal called for "serious consideration." The fact that the "plan" was not rejected out-of-hand reflects a strange ambivalence. . . .

The Soviet leadership may have sloughed off some of the ideological preconceptions which obstructed the pilot project of "socialism in one country." But the conflict strategy propounded by Lenin, refined by Stalin, and pressed with greater vigor and resourcefulness by his successor has not changed. It cannot change so long as Communist power is rivalled by Western power. It cannot change until Communism ceases to be itself.

. . . We have of late been exposed to

From Robert Strausz-Hupé, "The Disarmament Delusion," *U.S. Naval Institute Proceedings*, Vol. 86, No. 2 (February 1960), pp. 41–47. Copyright 1960 by the U.S. Naval Institute. Reprinted by permission.

the argument that the significance of the Soviet proposal lay precisely in the fact that it was uttered by a man who has broken with the past—that Khrushchev, having already courageously "liberated" Russia from Stalinist oppression, is willing to jettison the remaining Communist ideological ballast which encumbers a genuinely "peaceful coexistence."

This assumption is questionable.

Is total disarmament feasible? Ever since the introduction of the means of mass destruction, men of good will have fervently searched for a way to dispel the specter of conflict. It is understandable that World War II strengthened the desire for peace. The reasons are plain: the destructive power of armaments and their cost have grown and are growing far beyond anything envisaged in the halcyon years after World War I.

Yet even "peace-loving" nations continue to arm while insisting on the need for disarmament. Competitive armament between nations cannot be attributed, as many naïve souls thought after World War I, to the evil machinations of ambitious generals and greedy munitionsmakers. Armaments reflect the fears and ambitions of whole peoples and, ironically, their craving for economic security or prosperity. *Armaments are not the causes but the symptoms of conflict.*

Consequently, Khrushchev's proposal for total and universal disarmament slights the intelligence of anyone who has pondered the meaning of conflict. He is proposing, in effect, that not only the two super-powers and their allies forswear physical struggle, but that competing nations everywhere bury their differences. Will India and Pakistan scrap their arsenals as long as the status of Kashmir is in doubt? Will Israel and the Arab states accept disarmament as long as their views of the future of Palestine remain diametrically opposed?

But even if, by some miracle, political and ideological strife were suddenly to vanish from this earth and nations everywhere were to forego expansionist aims and suppress the instincts of self-protection, the problem of putting a universal program into effect staggers the imagination. It would mean a complex multitude of interlocking treaties, covenants, and agreements. It would mean a mammoth organization, with nerve centers in every area of the world. Finally, it would mean thousands of inspection teams, staffed by experts and provided with the most up-to-date scientific equipment. According to the Spanish philosopher and statesman, Salvador de Madariaga: "The problem of disarmament is not the problem of disarmament. It is really the problem of the organization of the World Community."

One of the major arguments in favor of disarmament is that it would lift the burdens which now weigh so heavily upon the economies of nations. A universal inspection system, even if it were feasible, would be a tremendously costly undertaking. This fact alone should not, of course, detract from the manifold blessings of disarmament. It should, however, serve to caution those who accept unquestioningly Khrushchev's picture of the plethora of material happiness and economic well-being which would automatically attend any disarmament scheme.

Can the Soviets accept a bona fide *inspection system?* All attempts, since 1948, at achieving agreement on an enforceable disarmament scheme have foundered on the Soviets' refusal to assent to any viable system of inspection.

The Soviets have refused to accept inspection for the same reason that they have refused to cease their jamming of foreign broadcasts beamed to Russia and the captive nations: they cannot significantly open Soviet society to the intrusion and scrutiny of outsiders without endangering the security of the regime and forfeiting important military assets in the global conflict.

Secrecy is a synonym of totalitarianism. A dictatorial regime can maintain itself in power only so long as it is able to insulate its dominion against the spread of "heretical" ideas and as long as it can keep the shutters drawn on windows which might afford its subjects a comparison of their fate with that of others. A "closed society" means just that—closed to the outside world.

Yet, secrecy has also an important military meaning. The German strategist von Schlieffen set forth the famous military dictum: "Be more than you seem." The Soviets have, in effect, reversed this prescription to read: "Seem more than you are." Soviet military might—other than that which is paraded annually before Lenin's Tomb on Red Square—has been a persistent enigma in the eyes of the world. Its very mystery has made it appear all the more sinister. Through deft showmanship and careful display, the Soviets have been able to elongate the shadow cast by power. Thus, they have parlayed their achievements in rocketry into smashing psychological victories precisely because the West does not know at what expense in resources and manpower and after how many failures these achievements were wrought.

The Soviets, in short, have monopolized the offensive in the global struggle from their vantage point of a monolithic, closed, secretive society. It is unlikely, to say the least, that they can appreciably open their territory to inspection—let alone scrap their physical power—without denying their ideological heritage, undermining their stability, and thus ceasing to be themselves.

This assertion may draw the now standard objections: Khrushchev has closed the book on Stalinism; the Soviet regime is "mellowing"; Soviet society is in an "era of transition." No one can deny that there have been changes in the Soviet Union—no society is completely static. But the import of "changes" in Russia has yet to be assessed. Suffice it to say that "liberalization" cannot be measured by the number of political prisoners released, by the bulk of tourist visas stamped by *Intourist,* or by the sale of *Amerika* at Soviet newsstands. There are limits to liberalization—limits of which Premier Khrushchev is perfectly aware. Whatever "changes" take place in Soviet society are ordained at the top: they cannot be exposed to external influences without endangering the very existence of the ruling hierarchy.

In short, so long as dictatorship endures in the Soviet Union, the Soviets cannot agree to broad inspection, because it would dangerously undermine the stability of the system—especially a system in transition. If, on the other hand, a truly democratic government would appear by some miracle in Russia, the utility of an inspection system would be considerably reduced because, presumably, such a government would not be aggressive. There is no middle solution.

Under present circumstances, what kind of inspection system are the Soviets likely to accept? Premier Khrushchev gave a clue to Soviet intentions in his speech to the United Nations when he differentiated between *bona fide* inspection functions and those which served as a cover for "intelligence activities." We can infer from this that, presumably, the

Soviets might allow, on a *quid pro quo* basis, visits to some selected installations which they might otherwise keep closed. Presumably, also, they would admit only inspection teams not staffed by "intelligence agents"—i.e., representatives of the Western powers. While such "concessions" might suffice in the eyes of those who want disarmament—real or symbolic, general or partial—at any cost, they would hardly provide the minimum condition on which a viable, self-enforcing arrangement must be based.

Can the Soviets disarm without abandoning political control of their empire? Despite the fact that some of the satellites are not effectively occupied by Soviet forces, the Soviet Union maintains its power in Central Europe largely by military means. Since it is extremely difficult to overthrow a well-armed dictatorship, especially one supported from the outside, it could be argued that, despite the Hungarian example, Communism can maintain itself in these states (except probably East Germany) even after Soviet troop withdrawal. The situation might be somewhat different if it were made clear that the Soviet military forces would not return. Moreover, the way in which this withdrawal would be brought about matters considerably. On balance, it can be said that the Soviets probably estimate that their military presence in at least some of the satellite countries, as well as easy military access to Central Europe, is an indispensable element of their rule over these nations, as well as a key factor in their over-all strategic position.

A mere *reduction* in the size of Soviet forces need not seriously weaken the Soviet grip on Central Europe. This depends in part on what type of forces they would retain. To the extent that, qualitatively as well as quantitatively, Soviet military strength really would be reduced and limited as to its deployment possibilities, the Soviet position in Central Europe would be weakened.

Khrushchev, in his proposal, was careful to draw the distinction between "armies, navies, and air forces," which would be disbanded, and "police" or "militia," which presumably would not. This distinction is a plausible one in the Western world in which, traditionally, policemen have patrolled the streets and soldiers have waged battle. The Western nations, with the possible exception of Hitler's Germany and its *Waffen* SS, have little experience in the potential of dual-purpose paramilitary forces.

In a totalitarian society, by contrast, military and police functions are merged inseparably. An important function of Red Army units and satellite military forces in Central Europe has been imperial control. Conversely, so-called "police" organizations in the Soviet Union have a distinctly military character. The MVD, for example, commands units armed with all the paraphernalia of conventional warfare. In the event of formal disarmament, Moscow could easily assign to "militias" the policing duties now carried out by Red Army and satellite forces.

There is another factor which must be considered in the relationship between disarmament and imperial control, namely, the psychology of the captive peoples. Revolution may erupt spontaneously, but its sustaining drive is the expectation of success. In the case of the satellites, this expectation hinges on the availability of outside help. It is doubtful, for example, whether the Hungarian Freedom Fighters, courageous though they were, would have taken up arms against the Soviets and their local satraps had it not been for the hope, however tragically misplaced, of Western assistance. The fact that this assistance was not forthcoming may have dampened such hope as may still linger among opponents of the various Communist regimes. If the West were completely disarmed, however, these remaining hopes would be completely extinguished.

Disarmament, therefore, may not necessarily mean the dissolution of the Soviet empire. But the hope that the Soviets, acting on this assumption, will agree to effective disarmament measures is fanciful. Moscow will not pay an excessive price for disarmament, and the very *possibility* that Communism in Central Europe will be eliminated would be an excessive price for the Soviets.

Would the Soviets, by sacrificing their armies, forfeit their hegemonial ambitions? The Soviets are masters at magnifying the psychological impact of physical power. Their unquestioned superiority in armed manpower has provided Communist conflict strategy and diplomacy with a formidable backstop. The Soviets, in Berlin and elsewhere, are leading through Western weakness—specifically weakness in conventional forces. So long as Communist gambits, such as the one in Berlin, compel the Western powers to contemplate the painful choice between all-out nuclear war and limited defeat, for just that long will Moscow be able to drive its psychological advantage home.

It is unlikely, to say the least, that the Soviets are ready to scrap this advantage in the interest of peace and universal well-being. Partial disarmament, incidentally, would not deprive them of this advantage. Power is relative, but its impact is absolute. If there were a proportionate cut in the conventional military might of the Soviet Union and that of its neighbors, Soviet power would still assert itself as before and the security problem confronting the Free World would be essentially unchanged.

But let us assume that the Soviets were willing to forego this advantage and accept total disarmament. Formal disarmament does not hold the same meaning for Soviet policy makers that it does for their opposites in the West. It does not for the simple reason that, while the West views conflict as the confrontation of organized military power, the Communist weapons spectrum scales the entire range of revolutionary conflict techniques. In this spectrum, conflict waged by irregular or "unconventional" forces—fifth columns and guerrillas—is assigned the same, if not greater, importance than that attached to massed armies and the launching pads of nuclear destruction. Indeed, since World War II, it is these conflict techniques which the Communists have used with almost unqualified success—in Central Europe, South Asia, and the Middle East. The Korean War was the only encounter which could be classed as a formal military conflict—and even this engagement abounded in such "unconventional" techniques as the use of proxies and "volunteers." No system of inspection and control could be devised which could conceivably ferret out every infiltrator, guerrilla band, or arms cache.

The argument could be raised that these considerations are extraneous to the central issue of disarmament: the Soviets enjoy this advantage today; why should they not continue to enjoy it if and when formal disarmament is implemented?

This argument overlooks some obvious facts. The West's military power, while it has not succeeded in halting the Communist machine of irregular conflict, has managed to brake it somewhat. It has done so in two ways. First, America's strategic power has forced the Communist conflict managers to proceed with circumspection in some areas, notably in Europe; the Soviets cannot be certain that any aggressive moves, no matter in what guise, in areas vital to American interests might not trigger America's strategic retaliation. Secondly, in those regions outside the West's immediate security zone, the so-called "grey areas," the build-up, with Western assistance, of local military and constabulary forces has raised considerably the security and morale of nations which would otherwise be an easy prey for diverse forms of Communist attack. Laos is a case in point. Were the American presence removed and were these local armies to be dissolved or even reduced, Communism's irregular warriors—its guerrilla bands and local party formations—could proceed virtually unchallenged.

Formal disarmament, therefore, would not halt Communist expansion. Indeed, it would widen immensely a battlefield in which the Communists are proven masters.

Can we rely on the Soviet Union to observe a disarmament agreement?

This is the crucial question. Amid the euphoria which attended Premier Khrushchev's tour through the United States, one central fact was generally neglected: according to all criteria of responsible government, Nikita S. Khrushchev is not the legitimate head of a legitimate government. Bolshevism ascended to power in Russia through violence. There is no orderly transfer of government in the Soviet Union—only a ruthless power struggle in which the victor is free—and, indeed, in the nature of the struggle, almost obliged—to scuttle the policies of his predecessors or vanquished opponent. Thus, Stalin stepped to power over the dead Lenin and the exiled Trotsky and substituted the goal of "socialism in one country" for the objective of immediate and global revolution. Thus, also, Khrushchev stepped to power over the dead Stalin, the murdered Beria, and the purged Molotov, Malenkov, and Kaganovich, and broke with the policies of the once "beloved" Soviet leader and "infallible" Communist theoretician, Comrade Stalin.

There is no guarantee that, even if Khrushchev is sincere, his successor will not disavow his policies and his commitments; indeed, Soviet precedent tells us that Khrushchev's heir, in order to emasculate the entourage of his departed or purged predecessor and to affirm his devotion to Communist orthodoxy, is likely to denounce a disarmament agreement concluded by his predecessor. Should then the Soviets decide to rearm, a mere inspection system will not prevent them from rescinding existing agreements. The inertia of the democracies, so vividly illustrated by their lethargy in the face of Hitler's unilateral scrapping of the Versailles Treaty, will make it extremely difficult, to say the least, to counter Communist rearmament.

In sum, the key to the problem of rearmament is the nature of the political systems that are parties to a disarmament agreement. The democracies can be relied upon to observe such an agreement, if only because their peoples abhor conflict and crave relief from the arms burden and, more important still because they can compel their government to comply with popular wishes and the agreements concluded in their name. No doubt, the Russian masses share the Western peoples' aversion to war and arming for war. Yet, they cannot force *their* leaders to comply with *their* wishes. And even if they had the power to force their leaders to lend a more willing ear to their desires, they lack the considerable information on the issues of war and peace which is available to every citizen of Western democracy.

The West cannot gamble its security on a disarmament agreement until it faces across the conference table men who represent an open political system, are responsive to the popular will, and have foresworn aggression. A disarmament agreement, like any other covenant, must be based on mutual confidence.

In 1928, the Sixth World Congress of the Communist International offered its member parties the following explanation of a disarmament proposal made by the Soviet Union to the Geneva Preparatory Conference in 1927: "The proposals for general and complete disarmament submitted by the Soviet Government . . . in November 1927 differ radically in aim, sincerity, and objective significance from the phrases and schemes submitted by the imperialists and their Social Democratic flunkeys. The aim of the Soviet proposals is not to spread pacifist illusions, but to destroy them; not to support capitalism by ignoring it or toning down its shady sides, but to propa-

gate the fundamental Marxian postulate, that disarmament and the abolition of war are possible only with the fall of capitalism. . . . It goes without saying, that not a single Communist thought for a moment that the imperialists would accept the Soviet disarmament proposals."

In the same resolution, the Communists defined what they consider to be a "peace policy," namely one "which conforms to the interest of the ruling class in Soviet Russia . . . and to the interest of the international proletariat. This policy rallies all the allies of the proletarian dictatorship around its banner and provides the best basis for taking advantage of the antagonisms among the imperialist States. The aim of this policy is to guard the international revolution. . . . The peace policy of the proletarian State certainly does not imply that the Soviet State has become reconciled with capitalism. . . . It is merely another—and under present conditions—a more advantageous form of fighting capitalism."

"Present conditions" are still advantageous. The "antagonisms" among the opponents of Communism are still strong. And the "peace policy" is all the more effective because it is waged in the shadow of Soviet power.

Thomas C. Schelling:
THE ROLE OF DETERRENCE
IN TOTAL DISARMAMENT

Thomas C. Schelling of the Center for International Affairs at Harvard University is an economist with a special concern for the study of bargaining. He has therefore been interested in the "theory of games," which involves the building of purely mathematical models of the kind of rational bargaining that would maximize the gains of bargainers who were in conflict with each other. But he has also tried to examine bargaining experimentally, has drawn from his experiments some conclusions about the nature of threats and promises in a strategy, and has tried to apply these conclusions to international strategy. His work has emphasized some of the seeming paradoxes that underlie effective strategy: for example, he has explored the use by rational men of deliberate irrationality in order to drive a better bargain, and here he explores what he believes would be the continued role of potentially military deterrence in the world of total disarmament.

A sharp distinction is often drawn between arms control and disarmament. The former seeks to reshape military incentives and capabilities; the latter, it is alleged, eliminates them. But the success of either depends on mutual deterrence. Short of universal brain surgery, nothing can erase the memory of weapons and how to build them. If "total disarmament" is to make war unlikely, it must reduce the incentives. It cannot eliminate the potential for destruction; the most primitive war can be modernized by rearmament as it goes along.

To determine whether and how disarmament might make war less likely we have to look at what the military opportunities, risks, dangers, fears, and potential capabilities would be in a disarmed world. If nations now suspect each other of contemplating war, we have to suppose that they might suspect each other of contemplating rearmament. If nations are willing to risk war, or to threaten it, they certainly might risk rearming or threatening to rearm. Nations thought capable now of being panicked into war might be panicked into rearmament. To suppose the contrary is to assume away the problem that disarmament is intended to help solve.

An international military authority is commonly proposed as a part of plans for total disarmament. It does make a difference whether or not we assume the existence of such an authority to police the otherwise disarmed world. But for the visible future it is a little extreme to suppose that an international force could contain or deter the United States and the Soviet Union; more than that, the concept poses problems of deterrence not wholly unlike those that would confront the major powers in a fully disarmed world. So we shall first consider universal disarmament without any international security force. And we shall assume a world disarmed to the levels proposed by those who favor the most drastic "total disarmament."

There are good reasons why this phrase should be set off in quotation marks. An obvious one is that there can be no absolute assurance that some nuclear weapons have not been kept. But, cheating aside, war can be waged with even the most primitive weapons, especially with the help of commercial aircraft, ships, trucks, radios, and the other paraphernalia of industrial society. More important, if war breaks out a nation can rearm unless its capacity is destroyed at the outset and kept destroyed. By the standards of 1944, the United States was fairly near to total disarmament when World War II broke out. Virtually all munitions later expended by United States forces were nonexistent in September 1939. "Disarmament" did not preclude U.S. participation; it just slowed it down.

As we eliminate weapons, warning systems, vehicles and bases, we change the criteria of military effectiveness. Airplanes are more important if missiles are banned; complex airplanes are needed less if complex defenses are banned. Since weapons themselves are the most urgent targets in war, to eliminate a weapon eliminates a target and changes the requirements for attack. At some stage in disarmament a donkey becomes a means of delivery, though we assume that "total" disarmament stops short of that.

The difficulty cannot be avoided by banning weapons of attack and keeping those of defense. If nations were large, self-sufficient islands, coast artillery might seem useless for aggression and valuable safeguards against war and the fear of war. But they are not; and in the present era, "defensive" weapons often embody equipment or technology that is superbly useful in attack and invasion. Moreover, a prerequisite of successful attack is some ability to defend against retaliation or counterattack. In a disarmed world, whatever lessens the scale of retaliation reduces the risk a nation runs in starting war. Defenses against retaliation thus are close substitutes for offensive power.

II. GENERAL WAR IN A DISARMED WORLD

Disarmament would not preclude the eruption of a crisis; war and rearmament could seem imminent. Even without possessing complex weapons, a nation might consider initiating war with whatever resources it had, on grounds that delay would allow an enemy to strike or mobilize first. If a nation believed its opponent might rush to rearm to achieve military preponderance, it might consider "preventive war" to forestall its opponent's dominance. Or, if confidence in the maintenance of disarmament were low and if war later under worse conditions seemed at all likely, there could be motives for "preventive ultimatums," or for winning a short war through coercion with illicitly retained nuclear weapons, or for using force to impose a more durable disarmament arrangement.

The decision to attack might be made reluctantly, motivated not by the prospective gains of victory but by the disadvantages of not seizing the initiative. Motives to undertake preventive or preemptive war might be as powerful under disarmament as with today's weapons—perhaps more powerful.

In a disarmed world, as now, the objective would probably be to destroy the enemy's ability to bring war into one's homeland, and to "win" sufficiently to prevent his subsequent build-up as a military menace. The urgent targets would be the enemy's available weapons of mass destruction (if any), his means of delivery, his equipment that could be quickly converted for strategic use, and the components, stand-by facilities, and cadres from which he could assemble a capability for strategic warfare.

Suppose both sides have violated the agreement and possess nuclear bombs at least in the scores or hundreds (or suppose the attacker has, and must anticipate that his opponent has). The attacker's first objective is to forestall the delivery of bombs in return. Compared with the present, the disarmed world would offer the attacker both advantages and disadvantages.

An advantage is that the time scale of attack may be more lenient. The victim may have a secret nuclear stockpile; but if he is unprepared it will take time to bring together, say, commercial aircraft, crews and the hidden nuclear weapons, and to improvise fueling arrangements and target plans. To do this in the hostile environment of even small-scale nuclear attack might be difficult. But the attacker would be coordinated rather than surprised and could make effective use of evacuation procedures or of any air defenses he could improvise.

If, instead, each side has plans for the contingency and maintains a "reserve force"—some part, say, of its commercial air fleet and crews—the victim of attack may react quickly. The attacker's own air defenses have been banned by agreement (and air defenses may be hard to conceal); in these conditions a retalia-

tory force of even low efficiency may be effective if it is large and dispersed.

If the aggressor has nuclear weapons and the victim does not, the latter's response will depend on how rapidly production can be resumed. Standby capacity may be available, or there may be nuclear facilities that can be converted to produce weapons. If these facilities have not been destroyed, the lag may be short, but a matter of days at least. Critically important would be the defenses, the dispersal or the secrecy of the facilities for producing nuclear materials or for assembling nuclear weapons. If the sites are few in number, of known location, above ground and without air defense, they would be destroyed before operations could be resumed. If the production facilities are in secret locations we may as well assume that nuclear weapons also exist.

III. A WAR OF NUCLEAR
MOBILIZATION

In the event that neither side had nuclear weapons, asymmetrical lead-times in nuclear rearmament could be decisive. Whether it took days or months, the side that believed it could be first to acquire a few dozen megatons through a crash rearmament program would expect to dominate its opponent. This advantage would be greatest if nuclear facilities themselves were vulnerable to nuclear bombardment: the first few weapons produced would be used to spoil the opponent's nuclear rearmament. Even if facilities are deep under the ground, well disguised or highly dispersed, a small difference in the time needed to acquire a few score megatons might make the war unendurable for the side that is behind. If one side appears likely to gain the decisive advantage, it might find "preventive rearmament" coupled with a surrender ultimatum an irresistibly attractive move.

It would not necessarily be essential to possess nuclear weapons in order to destroy nuclear facilities. High explosives, commandos or saboteurs could be effective. "Strategic warfare" might reach a purity not known in this century: like the king in chess, nuclear facilities would be the overriding objective. Their protection would have absolute claim on defense.

In such a war the object would be to preserve one's mobilization base and to destroy the enemy's. To win a war would not require overcoming the enemy's defenses—just winning the rearmament race. If commandos can bypass home defenses and paralyze the adversary's nuclear mobilization base, the jig is up—unless all participants can do this to each other. If they can, the prospect is for a bizarre kind of "broken-backed" war, bizarre because no back is broken, and the struggle to acquire nuclear weapons goes on—hopefully not too fast and too furiously to allow parallel negotiations for an agreed stalemate or a second try at "disarmament."

Another kind of warfare may emerge—"nuclear coercion." If an attacker possesses illicit nuclear weapons that can be dropped on a country that is unable to retaliate promptly, it might force a surrender through the destruction of cities and the threat of destroying more. Or the coercive campaign could combine preclusive destruction of the mobilization base with the demoralizing effects of concurrent civil damage. The expectation would be that, if significant rearmament could be retarded, capitulation would be forthcoming.

Such a war might be less destructive than war under present conditions, not primarily because disarmament had reduced the attacker's capability but because, with the victim unable to respond, the attacker could adopt a more measured pace that allowed time to negotiate a cease-fire before he had reduced his victim to rubble. Victory, of course, might be achieved without violence. If one side appears to have an advantage so convincingly decisive as to make the outcome of the war seem inevitable, it could then deliver an ultimatum instead of weapons.[1]

Disarmament might also cause nuclear weapons to be a greater equalizer among nations than they are now. A future Castro might be in a better position to plague or coerce the great powers by secreting nuclear weapons on his territory. In a world in which such forms of nuclear mischief have replaced the space-age machinery of war and in which the push-button has given way to improvised aerial ferries, the military environment may become less predictable and possibly more unstable.

To sum up: a stable military environment will not result automatically from a ban on weapons and the facilities to make them. The timing of war and rearmament, and the role of speed and initiative, will remain critically important in a world in which the pace of war is initially slowed. War may become more calculable and less fearsome. And there would remain, even in the design of "total disarmament," the difficult choice between minimizing war's destructiveness and minimizing its likelihood. If dis-

[1] Deterrence being largely a matter of credibility, it might not always be an advantage to have it believed that one is complying with the prohibition on nuclear weapons. At the slightest suspicion that others may be initiating preparations, a government might prefer to hint that it was already prepared. A small nuclear capability might be used to demonstrate a larger professed capability.

armament is to discourage the initiation of war and to remove the incentives toward preemptive and preventive war, it has to be *designed* to do that. Disarmament does not eliminate military potential; it changes it.

IV. LIMITED WAR IN A
DISARMED WORLD

While disarmament would eliminate the guns, it would not eliminate the trucks, aircraft, ships, communication equipment and canned food that are required for limited military campaigns. Nations could be expected to have plans for limited-war mobilization, including limited departures from the arms agreement itself.[2]

As important as the direct consequences that disarmament would have for limited war would be the indirect consequences. If disarmament reduces fears of general war—if explosion or escalation into general war seems a less likely prospect, or less disastrous if it should occur—the result may be fewer inhibitions on limited war. There could also be new restraints. If it is perceived that the outbreak of local wars may destroy the agreement itself—either through a sudden breakdown or steady erosion—this may create a determination to preserve what has been achieved and a recognition that to abandon restraints would signal "open season" on military competition. Of course, the more all parties value the climate of disarmament, the more can be gained by threatening to disturb it.

As "limited war" is possible, so is "limited violation" of disarmament. Since limits on hostilities can evidently be observed during war itself, limits on rear-

mament might be arrived at in similar fashion, even in the course of limited hostilities. The responses of countries not participating in the war would be important—perhaps an important brake, possibly a stimulus, on the resumed armament.

In limited war as in general war under conditions of "total disarmament," timing would be important. Offensive strategy in a limited war is often designed to achieve a *fait accompli*. Defense against this strategy in a disarmed world would depend on the ability of the defender (or protector) to rearm in time to repel or to stalemate the aggression. If we reflect on the critical timing of the North Korean invasion and the shortage of ammunition that plagued us throughout the whole Korean campaign, or the problems of the preemptive landing of Marines in Lebanon or the progress of the Suez campaign, it is evident that logistical considerations can be decisive. The likelihood that limited aggression will be deterred by the threat of limited rearmament may therefore depend on the mobilization speed that can be achieved from a standing start.

V. THE DETERRENCE OF REARMAMENT
IN A DISARMED WORLD

Many concepts that apply to the deterrence of war apply to deterrence of rearmament: "preventive" rearmament, "preemptive" rearmament, "escalation" of rearmament, "catalytic" rearmament, and rearmament stimulated by misinformation, misinterpretation, accident, false alarm, unauthorized conspiracy and other processes analogous to those that might trigger "inadvertent war" in an armed world. In addition, there are the possibilities of rearmament bubbling up out of a crisis, occurring in the course of

---

[2] The Chinese civil war of 1948–49 may illustrate how extensive a war can be fought with poor weaponry and primitive logistical support. Or the American Civil War.

a limited war or being undertaken by cool premeditation.

But despite the parallel, rearmament is not war. The fears, motives and moral attitudes that make initiation of war an opprobrious act do not apply with the same force to rearmament. The question whether to remain disarmed or to initiate limited rearmament could become a legitimate political issue. If the disarmament is so delicately balanced that there is great advantage in being the first to rearm, the mere existence of a political party pledged to abandon the disarmament treaty might disturb the arrangement. And to the extent that the treaty explicitly allows certain weapons or a mobilization base, continuing developments in technology will make armament, as well as disarmament, a proper topic of discussion and continuing negotiation.

The essential requirement is for some stable situation of "rearmament parity." If disarmament is to be durable, it must be apparent that the disadvantages of being behind in case an arms race should resume are not too great and that, in the face of ambiguous evidence of clandestine rearmament or overt evidence of imminent rearmament, nations can react without haste. The straightforward elimination of so-called "military production facilities" might, by sheer coincidence, provide the stability; but stability is more likely if there is a deliberately designed system of "stable equal readiness for rearmament." It is impossible to eliminate the ability to rearm; one can only hope to stretch the time required to reach, from the word "go," any specified level of rearmament. The problem is not *whether* to leave a mobilization base for rearmament, but what kind.

It is not certain that maximizing the time required to rearm is a way to deter it. Lengthening the racecourse does not necessarily lessen the incentive to be first under the wire. But it may reduce the advantage of a small head-start; it may allow time to renegotiate before the race has too much momentum; and it may reduce the confidence of a fast starter that he could win if he called for a race.

If rearmament is undertaken to improve mutual deterrence, not to achieve offensive superiority, it may not matter whether some nations fall behind. The leader will not necessarily race as fast as he can; for if he does, other nations may have to regard his behavior as a declaration of war and to respond accordingly. If a low-grade war of nuclear reprisal is within the capability of some laggard in the rearmament race, he may feel obliged to initiate such a war to disrupt another's rearmament; thus rearmament could lead to preemptive action and trigger a war. On the other hand, this prospect may help deter rearmament itself.

The likelihood of war, then, depends on the character of the disarmament. If mobilization potentials are such that a head-start is not decisive and the racecourse is long, preemptive action may be delayed until motives are clear. This, however, presents a dilemma analogous to that of deterring limited war today: the smaller the fear that rearmament will precipitate general war, the smaller the inhibition on rearmament.

Important elements for stability in a disarmed world would be the dispersal and duplication of standby facilities for rearmament and of reserve personnel or cadres around which rearmament can be mobilized. Dispersal is important because of the interaction between rearmament and war itself. If a nation can achieve just enough production of weapons to disrupt its opponent's rearmament, it may gain a decisive advantage. Once the race is on, a few easily-located facilities for producing nuclear weapons might invite a "preventive" and very limited war. If instead there were, say, scores or hundreds of laboratories able to produce unconventional weapons and if their destruction would require substantial military capabilities, there might be less incentive on one side to acquire and exploit a small advantage and less fear on the other of falling a little behind and being taken advantage of.

Nations are now willing to threaten war; in a disarmed world they certainly might threaten rearmament. The agreement itself would certainly have to be renegotiated from time to time, or continuously; and, just as a threat of "no sale" hangs over the head of commercial traders, so will the threat of rearmament hang over the heads of negotiators. The main sanction on the negotiations will be that, in the absence of a satisfactory agreement, nations may take unilateral steps for their own security or take steps to put pressure on others.

VI. ATTITUDES TOWARD REARMAMENT

The terms of an agreement must take into account what the attitude toward rearmament would be in the disarmed world. One approach would be that any overt rearmament would be a mortal sin, a total failure of the disarmament process, a contingency that can neither be planned for nor discussed coolly within countries or between governments. Alternatively, rearmament might be viewed as we view war now—as a tragedy and a failure of policy, but a tragedy that can occur, that can even occur from motives of self-defense, that can perhaps be limited and contained, and that need not signal the termination of all efforts at settlement and reconciliation.

The first attitude, which would try to insulate rearmament from the cold war and deprecate any planning for the contingency of rearmament, might be preferable if it could promise to create sufficiently strong inhibitions. If, instead, we have to expect—as surely we do—lapses under even the most ideal disarmament scheme, it is better to plan for such contingencies and to create the expectation that occasional lapses need not trigger a real arms race or the full fury of war itself. We cannot have it both ways. For if we recognize "limited rearmament" as a possibility and prepare for "limited responses" against it, we take some of the curse off rearmament, just as plans for limited war seem to legitimize war. This is a genuine dilemma.

Rearmament has other dimensions than speed and volume. We should distinguish between rearmament aimed at stable deterrence and rearmament aimed at brinkmanship or war. In this country we would certainly want to have careful rearmament plans so that, in the event we found ourselves unavoidably drawn into a renewed arms race, our actions would be consistent with deterrence of war and with an effort to slow down the pace of rearmament. The further rearmament goes and the more unstable the environment which it creates, the harder it will be to get back to the business of disarmament if we wish to.

It will also make a difference whether military and strategic planning is permitted and expected or frowned on. The dilemma is that stability will require careful planning of a kind inconsistent with the philosophy that military planning is illegal, immoral and a sign of evil intent. If nations suddenly awoke to rearmament dangers of which they had not been aware, their response might be more undisciplined and more unstable in the absence of military planning than if vigilance had been deliberately maintained.

It should not be expected that reduced tensions will be the natural consequence of a disarmament agreement. Not everyone will be confident that disarmament provides a viable military environment or promises the political atmosphere most conducive to peace and good relations. It is hard to believe that any sober person under any conceivable world arrangement could come to believe with confidence that war had at last been banished from human affairs until there had been at the very least some decades of experience. There will be surprises, rumors and sharp misunderstandings. Even if something that looks like "general and complete disarmament" is achieved, it is not out of the question that responsible governments might decide that international apprehensions would be reduced if they possessed more secure, more diversified and more professionally organized mobilization bases or weapon systems, with more freedom to improve them, drill them and discuss the strategy of their use.

It is even conceivable that a "rearmament agreement" would be negotiated in the interest of reducing tensions, the likelihood of war, the scope for "rearmament blackmail," the Nth-country problem, and perhaps even the economic costs of preparedness. It might be that moderate though expensive modern weapon systems, professionally organized and segregated from the main population centers, would provide less—not more—military interference in everyday life than a "total" disarmament agreement under which every commercial pilot carried emergency mobilization instructions in his briefcase. In any event, a decision on total disarmament, taken jointly by the major powers, would not bring an end to arguments about arms control.

VII. AN INTERNATIONAL MILITARY AUTHORITY

Some kind of international authority is generally proposed as part of an agreement on total disarmament. If militarily superior to any combination of national forces, an international force implies (or is) some form of world government. To call such an arrangement "disarmament" is about as oblique as to call the Constitution of the United States "a Treaty for Uniform Currency and Interstate Commerce." The authors of the Federalist Papers were under no illusion as to the far-reaching character of the institution they were discussing, and we should not be either. Here, however, we can focus only on those aspects of an International Force that directly affect the military environment.

One concept deserves mention in passing: that the projected police force should aim to control persons rather than nations. Its weapons would be squad cars, tear gas and pistols; its intelligence system would be phone taps, lie detectors and detectives; its mission would be to arrest people, not to threaten war on governments. Here, however, we shall concentrate on the concept of an International Force to police nations—and all nations, not just small ones. The most intriguing questions are those that relate to the Force's technique or strategy for deterring and containing the former nuclear powers.

The mission of the Force would be to police the world against war and rearmament. It might be authorized only to stop war; but some kinds of rearmament would be clear signals of war, obliging the Force to take action. There might be, explicitly or implicitly, a distinction between the kinds of rearmament that call for intervention and the kinds that are not hostile.

The operations of the Force raise a number of questions. Should it try to contain aggression locally, or to invade the aggressor countries (or all parties to the conflict) and to disable them militarily? Should it use long-range strategic weapons to disable the country militarily? Should it rely on the threat of massive punitive retaliation? Should it use the threat or, if necessary, the practice of limited nuclear reprisal as a coercive technique? In the case of rearmament, the choices would include invasion or threats of invasion, strategic warfare, reprisal or the threat of reprisal; "containment" could not forestall rearmament unless the country were vulnerable to blockade.

Is the Force intended to do the job itself or to head a world-wide alliance against transgressors? In case of aggression, is the victim to participate in his own defense? If the Indians take Tibet, or the Chinese encourage armed homesteading in Siberia, the Force would have to possess great manpower unless it was prepared to rely on nuclear weapons. A Force could not be maintained on a scale sufficient to "contain" such excursions by a nation with a large population unless it relied on the sudden mobilization of the rest of the world or on superior weaponry—nuclear weapons if the defense is to be confined to the area of incursion. But the use of such weapons to defend, for example, South Viet Nam against Chinese infiltrators, Western Europe against the Soviet bloc, East Ger-

many against West Germany, or Cuba against the United States, would be subject to the ordinary difficulties of employing nuclear weapons in populated areas. A country threatened by invasion might rather capitulate than be defended in that fashion. Moreover, the Force might require logistical facilities, infrastructure and occasional large-scale manœuvres in areas where it expects to be called upon. Keeping large forces stationed permanently along the Iron Curtain is a possibility, but not one that brings with it all the psychological benefits hoped for from disarmament.

A sizeable intervention of the Force between major powers is not, of course, something to be expected often in a disarmed world. Nevertheless, if the Force is conceived of as superseding Soviet and American reliance on their own nuclear capabilities, it needs to have some plausible capability to meet large-scale aggression; if it hasn't the major powers may still be deterred, but it is not the Force that deters them.

A capability for massive or measured nuclear punishment is probably the easiest attribute with which to equip the Force. But it is not evident that the Force could solve the problems of "credibility" or of collective decision any better than can the United States alone or NATO collectively at the present time. This does not mean that it could not solve them—just that they are not automatically solved when a treaty is signed. If the Force is itself stateless, it may have no "homeland" against which counterreprisal could be threatened by a transgressor nation; but if it is at all civilized, it will not be wholly immune to the counter-deterrent threats of a transgressor to create civil damage in other countries. These could be either explicit threats of reprisal or implicit threats of civil destruction collateral to the bombardment of the Force's own mobilization base. (The Force presumably produces or procures its weaponry in the industrial nations, and cannot be entirely housed in Antarctica, on the high seas or in outer space.)

If it should appear technically impossible to police the complete elimination of nuclear weapons, then we should have to assume that at least minimal stockpiles had been retained by the major powers. In that case, the Force might not be a great deal more than one additional deterrent force; it would not enjoy the military monopoly generally envisaged.

One concept needs to be disposed of—that the Force should be strong enough to defeat a coalition of aggressors but not so strong as to impose its will against universal opposition. Even if the world had only the weapons of Napoleon, the attempt to calculate such a delicate power balance would seem impossible. With concepts like preemption, retaliation and nuclear blackmail, any arithmetical solution is out of the question.

The knottiest strategic problem for an International Force would be to halt the unilateral rearmament of a major country. The credibility of its threat to employ nuclear weapons whenever some country renounces the agreement and begins to rearm itself would seem to be very low indeed.

The kind of rearmament would make a difference. If a major country openly arrived at a political decision to abandon the agreement and to recover the security it felt it had lost by starting to build a merely retaliatory capability and sizeable home-defense forces, it is hard to envisage a civilized International Force using weapons of mass destruction on a large scale to stop it. Limited

nuclear reprisals might be undertaken in an effort to discourage the transgressor from his purpose. But unless the rearmament program is accompanied by some overt aggressive moves, perhaps in limited war, the cool and restrained introduction of nuclear or other unconventional weapons into the country's population centers does not seem plausible, unless non-lethal chemical or biological weapons could be used.

Invasion might offer a more plausible sanction, perhaps with paratroops armed with small nuclear weapons for their own defense; their objective would be to paralyze the transgressor's government and mobilization. But if this should be considered the most feasible technique for preventing rearmament, we have to consider two implications. We have provided the Force a bloodless way of taking over national governments. And a preemptive invasion of this kind might require the Force to act with a speed and secrecy inconsistent with political safeguards.

There is also the question of what kinds of rearmament or political activity leading to rearmament should precipitate occupation by the Force. In our country, could the Republicans or Democrats campaign on a rearmament platform, go to the polls and win, wait to be inaugurated, denounce the agreement, and begin orderly rearmament? If the Force intervenes, should it do so after rearmament is begun, or after a party has introduced a rearmament resolution in Congress? The illustration suggests that one function of the Force, or the political body behind it, would be to attempt first to negotiate with a potential rearming country rather than to intervene abruptly at some point in these developments.

Again, the character of rearmament would make a difference. Suppose the President presented a well-designed plan to build an obviously second-strike retaliatory force of poor preemptive capability against either the International Force or other countries, but relatively secure from attack. If he justified it on the grounds that the current military environment was susceptible to sudden overturn by technological developments, political upheavals, irrepressible international antagonisms, the impotence of the Force for decisive intervention, the corruption or subversion of the Force, or other such reasons, then the authorization of a drastic intervention by the Force in the United States would be less likely than if the President ordered a crash program to assemble nuclear weapons, trained crews and long-range aircraft. It would make a considerable difference, too, whether rearmament occurred at a time of crisis, perhaps with a war going on, or in calmer times.

The point of all this is simply that even an International Military Authority with an acknowledged sole right in the possession of major weapons will have strategic problems that are not easy. This is, of course, aside from the even more severe problems of political control of the "executive branch" and "military establishment" of the world governing body. If we hope to turn all our international disputes over to a formal procedure of adjudication and to rely on an international military bureaucracy to enforce decisions, we are simply longing for government without politics. We are hoping for the luxury, which most of us enjoy municipally, of turning over our dirtiest jobs—especially those that require strong nerves—to some specialized employees. That works fairly well for burglary, but not so well for school integration, general strikes or Algerian independence. We may achieve it if we create a sufficiently potent and despotic ruling force; but then some of us would

have to turn around and start plotting civil war, and the Force's strategic problems would be only beginning.

VIII. CONCLUSION

This is not an essay against disarmament, even "total disarmament." It is simply a warning against the notion that there is any once-for-all solution to the problems of world peace and government. It is against the notion that if only disarmament is "total" enough, we can forget about deterrence and all that. It is against the notion that under "total" disarmament there is no military potential to be controlled, balanced or stabilized.

There should be no divorce between deterrence and disarmament. If disarmament is to work, it has got to improve deterrence and to stabilize deterrence. Until a much greater community of interest exists in the world than is likely in this generation, war will have to be made unprofitable. It cannot be made impossible.

It is sometimes argued that to perpetuate military deterrence is to settle for a peace based on fear. But the implied contrast between arms control and total disarmament is not persuasive. What would deter rearmament in a disarmed world, or small wars that may escalate into large ones, must be the apprehension of a resumed arms race and war. The extent of the "fear" involved in any arrangement—total disarmament, negotiated mutual deterrence, or anything else—is a function of confidence. If the consequences of transgression are plainly bad—bad for all parties, and little dependent on who transgresses first—we can take the consequences for granted and call it a "balance of prudence." What keeps us from stepping off a train before it stops is not "fear"; we just know better.

Walter Millis and James Real:
THE ABOLITION OF WAR

Walter Millis has been writing for a generation on the causes of a succession of wars fought by the United States; James Real is concerned with the interpretations of modern technology to the public. Here, under the auspices of the Center for the Study of Democratic Institutions, they have joined to discuss the impact of the new weapons on the institution of war. They conclude that war can now be abolished because the super-bombs have made war irrelevant to the political concerns for which it has traditionally been fought. They sketch out a demilitarized world in which clashes of national interests continue but are resolved by means other than war.

THE broad change in contemporary habits of thought and action required to make a demilitarized world possible can be rather simply summed up. It is merely that men everywhere should come to regard the war system—the system, that is, of organized war between the great modern power centers—as obsolete. This may seem to say less than that men should come to regard it as criminal or pathological or ultimately catastrophic; actually it is to say a good deal more. Most men already regard war as criminal or pathologic or ultimately catastrophic; but this has not helped us much with the war problem. As war comes to be regarded as *irrelevant*, the problem will approach solution. The criminal or pathological or catastrophic elements in our affairs are never irrelevant; by attaching such adjectives to them we proclaim our intense belief in their importance. In ancient societies (the same is true of modern ones as well) the violation of certain taboos was a major crime, and the enormity of the crime measured the importance the society attached to the observance of the taboo. With the passage of time and the changes in the cultural patterns, many taboos became obsolete. Their violation no longer seemed to matter, and the violation itself ceased to be criminal. As long as we look on war as a crime it will doubtless remain with us, in spite of Nuremberg trials and arguments over "war guilt." When we see the whole system as obsolete and useless, organized war will begin to go the way of the hereditary ruling class, or any other of the many human institutions and cultural patterns that have outlived their usefulness.

Unfortunately, for men to come to regard organized war as obsolete requires more drastic changes in cultural patterns and thought habits than for them to see it as criminal or pathological. The broad change subsumes many more specific ones. Men must, for example, abandon their habit of believing that the safety and survival of the national community depend upon its military power and military preparations. We already know that this is not the case—that massive accumulations of military power in a nuclear age are far more likely to destroy than to conserve the national community. But we have as yet been unable to bring ourselves to *believe* this. Most of us are still unable to grasp the fact that the senseless question, "Would you rather be Red or dead?" is indeed senseless. It permits of no answer because its terms correspond to nothing in the contemporary international world; it has a purely emotional impact upon us because it summons up ideas or notions about the way in which the international world operates that are completely erroneous. It is senseless here; corresponding questions when asked in Russia or China are equally senseless, and men everywhere must alter their ideas to the extent necessary for them to realize it.

Men must abandon the idea that the surviving military institutions in one great state are in themselves a direct threat to other states. They must, to put it in another way, come to realize that the Soviet megaton bombs are as useless, in the long run, to the Soviet state as our own megaton bombs are to us. This realization is amply sustainable from the actual history of the past fifteen years, and seems to be more and more clearly demonstrable in events as time goes on. As the conclusion more clearly emerges, it will permit us and the other great military powers to make considerably greater contributions toward eventual demilitarization than we seem able to do now. We do not believe that we can now practically, or perhaps even safely, embark upon complete unilateral disarmament. We might, as was earlier suggested, go a good deal further in bowing out of the arms race than we now dare to do. We could accept test bans or similar disarmament beginnings on a much lower level of inspection and verification than we now feel it necessary to demand. If the institution is really, in our minds, obsolete and meaningless, one need take correspondingly lesser precautions against its possible revival—not, it must once more be insisted, because we come to "trust" the Russians or the Chinese but because we see no advantage to them in reviving it.

There are other established concepts that men must be willing to surrender if a demilitarized world is to be achieved. One of the most important, probably, is the myth of organized war as essential to the unity, the purpose, the "soul" of the state. We now believe that men must be willing to die for the state if the state is to survive ("Would you rather be Red or dead?"), just as it was once believed that they had to be willing to die at the stake for their religion if truth was to prevail. The great apparatus of military ritual, of the military uniform, of obeisance to the flag, of military training and obedience, is thought to be essential to the maintenance of a national unity and purpose—and it is thought that these must be sealed by the possibility of blood sacrifice if they are to retain their magical social power. In any society, democratic or dictatorial, the army remains the highest, most solemn expression of dedication to the common purpose, and many nation-states today, which find themselves under no significant external threat whatever, are reluctant to abandon military establishments that serve so many purposes of internal cohesion. Yet there are several smaller ones that have done so, without adverse result; and the argument ignores the successful history of other modern states that have not for decades or even centuries been involved in war.

Men must abandon the idea that either the great nuclear arsenals or the huge conventional military establishments maintained in the great power centers—the United States and Western Europe, Russia, China—are going to affect very greatly the future of world history. At the cost of untold agony and loss of life, we have now reached a position in which about two-thirds of the inhabitants of the world live in these four or five stabilized political-social organizations, each well ordered, largely self-sufficient, self-confident, and each incapable of seriously affecting the destiny of the others through warfare except at the price of suicide. Of these two-thirds of the globe's peoples, one is organized on mainly Western-democratic lines and the other on mainly Communist lines. Whether the masses in the "free world" are, on balance, happier or more productive or more content with their lot than the masses in the "unfree" world seems a somewhat academic question. But one thing can be said with certainty. That is, that neither the megaton arsenals nor the tank divisions are going to resolve such questions. Two world wars succeeded in churning up the human organization of the globe as it existed in 1910, with results which were in some ways beneficial as well as lamentable. A third war holds out no hope of any beneficial results whatever. A third world war can produce a universal catastrophe; short of that, the material needs, the political relations, the ambitions of the great power centers are not going to be significantly affected by their military establishments; war of this kind is already obsolete, and must sooner or later be recognized to be so.

There remains another third of the global population, more or less, in a state of relative instability, change, and revolution. In their efforts to control or channel developments in this huge area, the relatively stable great-power centers are in rivalry. They are not, it must be insisted, in a state of war (the "cold war" has always been a misleading analogy), and their weaponry is unlikely to be of much effect. The great powers have not in fact deployed their armaments in this area since 1945. Even in Korea, the closest approach during this period to a resort to the organized war system, the United States used only a small fraction of its total military power. The fourfold increase in 1950 in the American military budget went for the most part toward averting the supposed danger of a war in Europe, not toward winning the actual war in Korea. The position was strikingly different from that presented by the Russo-Japanese War of 1904–1905, in which both sides really strained themselves to the limit to achieve a conventional military victory.

In Indochina and in Algeria the French may have committed a relatively greater proportion of their military resources to victory; in neither case, however, did they make a total commitment comparable to that of 1914 or 1939, while these were both guerrilla wars in which "victory" on the old pattern was essentially impossible. "The object of war," as General MacArthur (in one of his many moods) once sonorously declared, "is victory." This was roughly true of the war system as it operated in Western international relations through the past three centuries. Recognizable, clear-cut "victory" was as essential to the successful working of the system as accountable money profits are essential to the operation of a capitalist economic system. "Victory," accepted by both contestants, was the key to the whole business. But guerrilla war is fundamentally a denial that military victory matters—it is a denial of the very idea of victory; and the fact that wherever, since 1945, armed violence has significantly affected the social, political, and power relations of peoples it has almost exclusively taken the form of guerrilla warfare is one of the more striking of our demonstrations of the obsolescence of the organized war system.

It will never, presumably, be possible to eliminate armed violence, with its concomitants of manslaughter, from human affairs. What does seem possible, and indeed probable, is the elimination of the ritual organization of violence into forms that seem to ensure the slaughter of men by the tens or hundreds of millions. In considering this possibility, the resurgence of mob violence and guerrilla warfare as effective (if in themselves far from pretty) modes in the adjustment of international group relations is of the utmost interest. Guerrilla war has seldom, if ever, ended in anything like a recognizable "victory" on the old pattern. The outcome may register shifts in power, often very great shifts in power, but usually has the appearance of a compromise rather than of "victory." Guerrilla wars may succeed (as in Ireland in the 1920's) or fail (as in the Philippines after 1899), but whatever the outcome they usually leave an effect upon the future that it is difficult to describe by either the term "victory" or "defeat." They observe discernible laws that do not apply to the great organized conflicts between highly armed states. These laws are only beginning to receive the attention they deserve.

Regarded as a form of politics, there are two aspects of guerrilla war that are of particular interest. One is that it cannot survive unless it has behind it a large measure of popular support. In this, it represents a kind of crude popular referendum; but how far the affirmative "votes" are given because of hope, because of fear, because of terror, is usually as obscure as are the reasons why affirmative votes are given in more sophisticated electoral processes. The other interesting aspect of guerrilla war is the fact that it usually cannot succeed without outside support. Normally, it must have outside sources of money and weapons, safe bases for recruitment, training, and hospitalization of casualties. While the rule may not be invariable, there are many instances to sustain it. Perhaps it is enough to compare Cuba's ten-year "War of Independence" in 1868–1878, which failed because no one outside was greatly interested in it, with the second war for independence, which, beginning in 1895, succeeded brilliantly because of the immense emotional, logistic, and finally military support the United States put behind it.

In the first aspect, guerrilla war represents something like a popular referendum. In the second aspect, unhappily, it represents something like a vicarious great-power contest. As we ought to realize by now, it is not just the Russians or the Chinese who back their own sides in such contests; the United States and other Western powers have long been accustomed to doing the same. In the less stable areas of the world, guerrilla war is likely to represent *both* a popular referendum and a great-nation power conflict. It is hard to separate the values involved. The fact appears to remain, however, that the results yielded by power contests of this kind are normally accepted as final both for the internal power struggle they represent and for the external great-power struggle that may be at issue. It is today the settled policy of the United States to provide the South

Vietnamese with all the logistic and advisory support they may be able to use, but not to try to fight their war for them. Unless the Vietnamese can save themselves from the Communist pressure, the United States will not try to save them on its own initiative. What this seems to imply is that whereas the issue of Western as against Communist control of South Vietnam is important, it is not important enough for a major war and not so important that it cannot be left to decision by the complex factors on the ground. As a means of "saving" South Vietnam from Communism, the major-war system is obsolete; but the issue itself is not so tragic that it cannot reasonably be left to the lesser instrumentalities of power that are available.

To say, as has been said above, that men must abandon the idea that the existing hypertrophied armaments of the great powers are going to affect the future history of the world materially is to say that they must come to understand that there are alternative ways in which the world's power struggles can be (as they are being) conducted. They must come to realize that neither the thermonuclear holocaust itself nor the continued threat of it is in any way essential to a reasonably viable and rational adjustment of the world's power problems. To accept this is not to condemn the demilitarized world to an endless succession of guerrilla "wars of liberation" or violent riots, competitively fomented by the stable powers. The rise of mob violence and guerrilla war in the contemporary world is only one way in which the immensely complex problems of power are being resolved. It is in only rather small areas of the world, after all, that violence of this kind is significant in international affairs today; in a world demilitarized to police-force levels, the power problems themselves are certain to take on different forms. For the present argument, it is enough to say that for the demilitarized world to come into existence, men everywhere must come to regard the massive nuclear and conventional military establishments of the great states as irrelevant to the real problems of power. . . .

Once the world has been demilitarized, supranational authority will be needed primarily to ensure that rearmament does not take place; that the national police forces do not gradually develop into military threats against each other; and to exert in the less stable areas of the globe the kind of police power the UN has already been called upon to supply in Palestine and Africa. That it would have to establish compulsory enforceable jurisdiction in the settlement of "disputes" between the great powers seems doubtful. Once the enormous weapons systems, with the fears and the insoluble issues of abstract power that surround them, have been eliminated, differences that will continue to arise between the great-power centers will surely be susceptible to resolution by existing negotiatory and arbitral processes, as they are now within the Western community.

For all these purposes the supranational authority will have a modicum of armed force under its own veto-free command. It would not need and could not have a great supranational nuclear military force capable of coercing any of the great states—upon whose assent its own existence and effectiveness would depend. The whole success of a demilitarized world turns upon the *abolition* of military coercion as a means of adjusting the relations of states, and one cannot hope to abolish it on the national level if one is simply to reassemble it on the international level. The international police force, which appears in all plans for disarmament, must be just that—a police force and not an army. In the prevention of rearmament, most of the political and psychological factors will be, as has been suggested, on the side of the authority, and its useful instruments will be those of investigation, intelligence, and report, not of armed might. Once the world has been demilitarized, it is believed that it will be possible to define certain kinds of incitations or conspiracies looking toward clandestine rearmament or weapons development as international crimes, and to give the supranational police rights to intervene against such actions similar to those the American federal police organs enjoy within the several states. But by and large the great, highly organized powers can be relied upon to police themselves, as we now rely, for example, upon the great powers in NATO.

The functions and empowerment of the supranational police in the less stable areas of the globe are less easy to envisage. Since Theodore Roosevelt's claim to a "police power" in the Caribbean, if not long before, the idea of an international, or at least great-state, police control over "the little bandit nations" has been prominent in the discourse; but it has never been logically developed, and attempts to give it practical expression have rarely been happy. Khrushchev has cavalierly cut through the dilemma by saying that it will be the function of the international police to prevent all wars "except those of national liberation." The indignation with which this has been received in the West conceals the fact that the West (unless it really proposes to establish an iron *status quo* upon the globe) has no better answer for the riots, rebellions, and

guerrilla wars that would be fairly certain to continue in a world generally demilitarized. Where the limits of supranational authority (and supranational armed power) in such situations are likely to lie is a problem that calls for much more study than it has been given.

One can only say that we have, on the one hand, been learning by experience (for proof one need only compare the "UN police action" in Korea with those in Palestine and the Congo); while, on the other hand, the problem of local violence, rebellion, and guerrilla war will lose much of its dangerous significance in a generally demilitarized world. Local power conflicts may be anything but bloodless (though we tend to forget how many problems have been solved since 1945, how many vast changes have been effected, by substantially bloodless means) and may, as in Algeria or the Congo, present appalling pictures of injustice, cruelty, and disorder. But they are not "causes" of major war; they can at most only trigger a major war already prepared by other military and power factors. The notion that armed violence or even small-scale international war anywhere represents a kind of center of infection, capable, unless immediately suppressed, of spreading into a Third World War, stands the real processes of international politics on their head. The small war cannot explode into a great one unless the great one already stands ready for detonation. The small war is like the dynamite cap. The dynamite cap is in itself by no means harmless, and has to be handled with care to avoid local damage. But unless and until the dynamite is attached to it, the damage will remain localized.

For the time being, at least, the great powers have been effectively demilitarized by their own weaponry; a great war seems as of today impracticable, and is not in preparation. The great powers have eschewed direct military intervention in African issues, and the police problem has fallen more or less by default to the UN. The forces it has deployed are very small; they have not attempted to resolve the political and power issues involved, but have mainly tried only to limit the violence. This situation, it would seem, would be the same whether the great powers are temporarily demilitarized by fear of their own weaponry or permanently demilitarized by a *détente* and disarmament. The working results, in the Congo and elsewhere, have been disagreeable in the extreme; but they have not been catastrophic. It is hard to doubt that this experience provides a model for the probable function of a supranational police force in dealing with the remaining violence in a world generally disarmed.

The demilitarized world will not and cannot eliminate the infinite variety of power struggles inherent in the nature of man. What it can and must do is to eliminate the war system, under which all these struggles "head up," both needlessly and catastrophically, into a giant military struggle between four or five great centers of organized power. Mortal combat (especially mortal combat raised to levels of mass destruction hitherto practiced only in the ancient world) is not the only, it is not the usual, and it is not the final or even effective test of power in the modern world. There are many other ways besides organized war available today for resolving the almost infinite variety of power issues with which humanity must struggle. It is impossible to say with any precision just how these many issues would be dealt with in the absence of the great weapons systems; it is not impossible to prophecy that they would be dealt with much better than the weapons systems are likely to do. It is enough, for the moment, to point to the essential viability of a global system built upon the four or five great national power centers that now exist, these being mutually demilitarized to police-force levels and provided with a modicum of supranational force to ensure that no remilitarization took place and to provide for at least a minimum of order in the less stable areas of the world. . . .

J. William Fulbright:

THE COLD WAR
IN AMERICAN LIFE

*The whole set of assumptions underlying the Cold War as an inter-
national activity and the impact of that activity on democracy in America, were called into question by Senator J. William Fulbright of Arkan-
sas, chairman of the Senate Committee on Foreign Relations, in an address delivered early in 1964 at the University of North Carolina. In that
address he argued that a quarter-century of preoccupation with foreign
affairs might now be ending, and that the domestic needs of the United
States were coming back into focus as the prime concern of the American people. The interest aroused by his analysis has served to focus
attention upon the relation between thermonuclear strategy and future
political directions for the United States and the world at large.*

THE Constitution of the United States,
in the words of its preamble, was
established, among other reasons, in
order to "provide for the common defense, promote the general welfare, and
secure the blessings of liberty." In the
past generation the emphasis of our
public policy has been heavily weighted
on measures for the common defense to
the considerable neglect of programs for
promoting the liberty and welfare of our
people. The reason for this, of course,
has been the exacting demands of two
World Wars and an intractable cold
war, which have wrought vast changes
in the character of American life.

Of all the changes in American life
wrought by the cold war, the most important by far, in my opinion, has been
the massive diversion of energy and resources from the creative pursuits of civilized society to the conduct of a costly
and interminable struggle for world

power. We have been compelled, or
have felt ourselves compelled, to reverse
the traditional order of our national
priorities, relegating individual and
community life to places on the scale
below the enormously expensive military
and space activities that constitute our
program of national security.

This of course is not the only change
in American life brought about by the
cold war. There have been many others,
some most welcome and constructive.
Directly or indirectly, the world struggle
with communism has stimulated economic and industrial expansion, accelerated the pace of intellectual inquiry and
scientific discovery, broken the shell of
American isolation and greatly increased
public knowledge and awareness of the
world outside the United States. . . .

Overriding all these changes, however,
good and bad, has been the massive diversion of wealth and talent from indi-

Speech delivered at the University of North Carolina 1964 Symposium: "Arms and the Man:
National Security and the Aims of a Free Society." Reprinted by permission of the author from
the *Congressional Record*, April 7, 1964.

vidual and community life to the increasingly complex and costly effort to maintain a minimum level of national security in a world in which no nation can be immune from the threat of sudden catastrophe. We have had to turn away from our hopes in order to concentrate on our fears and the result has been accumulating neglect of those things which bring happiness and beauty and fulfillment into our lives. The "public happiness," in August Heckscher's term, has become a luxury to be postponed to some distant day when the dangers that now beset us will have disappeared.

This, I think, is the real meaning of the cold war in American life. It has consumed money and time and talent that could otherwise be used to build schools and homes and hospitals, to remove the blight of ugliness that is spreading over the cities and highways of America, and to overcome the poverty and hopelessness that afflict the lives of one-fifth of the people in an otherwise affluent society. It has put a high premium on avoiding innovation at home because new programs involve controversy as well as expense and it is felt that we cannot afford domestic divisions at a time when external challenges require us to maintain the highest possible degree of national unity. Far more pervasively than the United Nations or the "Atlantic community" could ever do, the cold war has encroached upon our sovereignty; it has given the Russians the major voice in determining what proportion of our Federal budget must be allocated to the military and what proportion, therefore, cannot be made available for domestic social and economic projects. This is the price that we have been paying for the cold war and it has been a high price indeed.

At least as striking as the inversion of priorities which the cold war has enforced upon American life is the readiness with which the American people have consented to defer programs for their welfare and happiness in favor of costly military and space programs. Indeed, if the Congress accurately reflects the temper of the country, then the American people are not only willing, they are eager, to sacrifice education and urban renewal and public health programs—to say nothing of foreign aid—to the requirements of the Armed Forces and the space agency. There is indeed a most striking paradox in the fact that military budgets of over $50 billion are adopted by the Congress after only perfunctory debate, while domestic education and welfare programs involving sums which are mere fractions of the military budget are painstakingly examined and then either considerably reduced or rejected outright. I sometimes suspect that in its zeal for armaments at the expense of education and welfare the Congress tends to overrepresent those of our citizens who are extraordinarily agitated about national security and extraordinarily vigorous about making their agitation known.

It may be that the people and their representatives are making a carefully reasoned sacrifice of welfare to security. It may be, but I doubt it. The sacrifice is made so eagerly as to cause one to suspect that it is fairly painless, that indeed the American people prefer military rockets to public schools and flights to the moon to urban renewal. In a perverse way, we have grown rather attached to the cold war. It occupies us with a stirring and seemingly clear and simple challenge from outside and diverts us from problems here at home which many Americans would rather not try to solve, some because they find domestic problems tedious and pedestrian, others because they genuinely believe these problems to be personal rather than public, others because they are unwilling to be drawn into an abrasive national debate as to whether poverty, unemployment, and inadequate education are in fact national rather than local or individual concerns.

The cold war, it seems clear, is an excuse as well as a genuine cause for the diversion of our energies from domestic well-being to external security. We have been preoccupied with foreign affairs for 25 years, and while striking progress has been made in certain areas of our national life, the agenda of neglect has grown steadily longer. We can no longer afford to defer problems of slums and crime and poverty and inadequate education until some more tranquil time in the future. These problems have become urgent if not intolerable in an affluent society. It is entirely reasonable to defer domestic programs in time of an all-out national effort such as World War II, but in the present cold war it is not reasonable to defer our domestic needs until more tranquil times, for the simple reason that there may be no more tranquil times in this generation or in this century.

In the long run, the solution of our domestic problems has as vital a bearing on the success of our foreign policies as on the public happiness at home. We must therefore reassess the priorities of our public policy, with a view to redressing the disproportion between our military and space efforts on the one hand and our education and human welfare programs on the other. We must distinguish between necessity and preference in our preoccupation with national security, judging our military needs

by a standard which takes due account of the fact that armaments are only one aspect of national security. . . .

The single-minded dedication with which we Americans have committed ourselves to the struggle with communism is a manifestation of a national tendency to interpret problems in moral and absolutist terms. We are, as Louis Hartz has pointed out, a Nation which was "born free." Having experienced almost none of the anguished conflict between radicalism and reaction that has characterized European politics, we have been virtually unanimous in our adherence to the basic values of liberal democracy. We have come to identify these values with the institutional forms which they take in American society and have regarded both as having moral validity not only for ourselves but for the entire world. We have therefore been greatly shocked since our emergence as a world power to find ourselves confronted with revolutionary ideologies which reject the faith in individual liberty and limited government that has served our own society so well.

Because of these predilections, the cold war has seemed to represent a profound challenge to our moral principles as well as to our security and other national interests. We have responded by treating Communist ideology itself, as distinguished from the physical power and expansionist policies of Communist states, as a grave threat to the free world. The cold war, as a result, has been a more dangerous, costly, and irreconcilable conflict than it would be if we and the Communist states confined it to those issues that involve the security and vital interests of the rival power blocs.

The ideological element in the cold war, reinforced by the moralist tendencies of the American people, has also had the effect of making the world conflict a much more disruptive element in American life than it would be if it were regarded primarily in terms of its effect on our national security. To an extent, the issue between the Communist and the free worlds is moral and ideological, but ideas and principles in themselves threaten no nation's vital interests except insofar as they are implemented in national policies. It is the latter, therefore, that are our proper concern. To the extent that we are able to remove the crusading spirit and the passions of ideology from the cold war, we can reduce its danger and intensity and relax its powerful hold on the minds and hearts of our people.

The fears and passions of ideological conflict have diverted the minds and energies of our people from the constructive tasks of a free society to a morbid preoccupation with the dangers of Communist aggression abroad and subversion and disloyalty at home. The problem did not end with the McCarthy era of a decade ago nor is it confined to the neurotic fantasies of today's radical right. The cold war malady affects a much broader spectrum of American society. It affects millions of sensible and intelligent citizens whose genuine concern with national security has persuaded them that the prosecution of the cold war is our only truly essential national responsibility, that missiles and nuclear armaments and space flights are so vital to the safety of the Nation that it is almost unpatriotic to question their cost and their proliferation, and that in the face of these necessities the internal requirements of the country—with respect to its schools and cities and public services—must be left for action at some remote time in the future—as if these requirements were not themselves vital to

the national security, and as if, indeed, our generation is likely to know more tranquil days.

In the 1830's Alexis de Tocqueville saw America as a nation with a passion for peace, one in which the "principle of equality," which made it possible for a man to improve his status rapidly in civilian life, made it most unlikely that many Americans would ever be drawn to form a professional military caste. In 1961, President Eisenhower warned the Nation of the pervasive and growing power of a "military-industrial complex." Tocqueville was quite right in his judgment that the United States was unlikely to become a militarist society. We have, however, as a result of worldwide involvements and responsibilities, become a great military power, with a vast military establishment that absorbs over half of our Federal budget, profoundly influences the Nation's economy, and exercises a gradually expanding influence on public attitudes and policies.

. . . Like any other piece of machinery, our Military Establishment can be no better than the judgment of those who control it. In a democracy, control is intended to be exercised by the people and their elected representatives. To a very considerable extent the American people are not now exercising effective control over the Armed Forces; nor indeed is the Congress, despite its primary constitutional responsibility in this field. Partly because of anxieties about the cold war, partly because of our natural technological bias, which leads us to place extraordinary faith in the ability of technicians to deal with matters that we ourselves find incomprehensible, and partly because of the vested interests of the military-industrial complex, we are permitting the vast Military Establishment largely to run itself, to determine its own needs, and to tell us what sacrifices are expected of us to sustain the national arsenal of weapons.

David Lloyd George once declared that "there is no greater fatuity than a political judgment dressed in a military uniform." To the extent that the American people and the Congress shrink from questioning the size and cost of our Defense Establishment, they are permitting military men, with their highly specialized viewpoints, to make political judgments of the greatest importance regarding the priorities of public policy and the allocation of public funds.

The abnegation of responsibility by the Congress in this field is strikingly illustrated by its debates or, more accurately, nondebates, on the defense budget. When, for example, Senator McGovern, of South Dakota, suggested last September that Defense spending might be reduced by 5 percent, the Senate, with virtually no discussion, voted the McGovern amendment down by a vote of 70 to 2 and proceeded, after an afternoon of desultory discussion, to enact the whole Defense appropriation bill. When, later in the fall, I had the dubious honor of managing the foreign aid bill on the Senate floor through 3 weeks of extremely contentious debate, I could not help noting how astonishingly the forces of economy had picked up strength between the debate on the $50 billion Defense appropriation and the $4 billion foreign aid bill. . . .

Many Americans may regard huge military and space programs as the only truly urgent requirements on our national agenda, but it is difficult to believe that this enthusiasm is shared by the 4.2 million Americans who are unemployed or by the 30 million Americans who have incomes of less than $3,000 a year.

While the cold war and our enormous-

ly costly national security programs preempt so much of our time and attention and national wealth, the most important resources of our country—its human resources—are being extravagantly wasted and neglected. As the President's recently issued Manpower report points out, unemployment in 1963 increased to 5.7 percent of the labor force despite major advances in production and employment; unemployment of young workers, between the ages of 16 and 19, reached 17 percent in 1963 while unemployment among nonwhite Americans stood at 11 percent; despite an unemployment rate twice as high for school dropouts as for high school graduates, 30 percent of all young people continue to end their education before completing high school; despite the decline in unskilled jobs and the expanding demand for professional, technical, clerical, and service workers—for workers, that is, with at least high school education and specialized training—nearly a million young people are leaving school every year without having completed elementary or secondary school. . . .

The statistics of poverty, though striking, are antiseptic compared to the actual misery and hopelessness of being poor. The real meaning of poverty is not just losses of learning and productivity, but thousands of angry and dispossessed teenagers who make our city streets dangerous for "respectable" citizens; 350,000 youngsters across the Nation who form what the Secretary of Labor has described as an "outlaw pack" because they have stopped looking for work, are unemployed today, and will remain so for the rest of their lives; children in a blighted mining town in eastern Kentucky who are potbellied and anemic from lack of food; sharecroppers, white as well as black, living in squalid shacks and working for a few dollars a day—when they can find work at all —anywhere in a crescent of rural poverty that extends from southern Virginia along the Coastal Plain across Georgia and Alabama into the Mississippi Delta and the Ozarks.

Poverty in America has a radically different moral connotation from poverty in underdeveloped nations. The poor countries of the world have the excuse, for what it is worth, that the means of feeding, housing, and educating their people simply do not exist. In America the means do exist; the failure is essentially one of distribution. The children who go to bed hungry in a Harlem slum or a West Virginia mining town are not being deprived because no food can be found to give them; they are going to bed hungry because, despite all our miracles

of invention and production, we have not yet found a way to make the necessities of life available to all of our citizens— including those whose failure is not a lack of personal industry or initiative but only an unwise choice of parents. . . .

If there is any validity in this analysis, then it follows that the first thing we must do toward raising the quality of American life is to turn some part of our thoughts and our creative energies away from the cold war that has engaged them for so long back in on America itself. If we do this, and then let nature take its course, we may find that the most vital resources of our Nation, for its public happiness and its security as well, remain locked within our own frontiers, in our cities and in our countryside, in our work and in our leisure, in the hearts and minds of our people.

Suggestions for Additional Reading

One effort to describe, categorize, and criticize recent strategic thought has been made by Robert A. Levine in *The Arms Debate* (Cambridge, 1963). But there have been serious objections to Levine's method and conclusions, and those who read his book should also see the reviews by Marcus G. Raskin in *The New York Review of Books* for November 14, 1963 (and the exchange of letters between Albert Wohlstetter and Raskin in the following issue, November 28, 1963); by Arthur I. Waskow in *Frontier*, October, 1963; and by Philip Green in *World Politics*, July, 1964.

The nature and effects of thermonuclear weapons are discussed by Samuel Glasstone, ed., *The Effects of Nuclear Weapons* (Washington, 1962); Ralph Lapp, *Kill and Overkill* (New York, 1962), and Tom Stonier, *Nuclear Disaster* (Cleveland, 1964). A useful, and occasionally sardonic, glossary of terms often used in nuclear material is provided by Donald M. Kaplan and Armand Schwerner, *The Domesday Dictionary* (New York, 1963).

For defenses of each of the three major thermonuclear strategies, see the following: for controlled thermonuclear war, Herman Kahn, *On Thermonuclear War* (Princeton, 1960) and *Thinking About the Unthinkable* (New York, 1962) and Richard Fryklund, *100 Million Lives* (New York, 1962); for minimal deterrence, Oskar Morgenstern, *The Question of National Defense* (New York, 1959), Henry A. Kissinger, *The Necessity for Choice* (New York, 1960), and George E. Lowe, *The Age of Deterrence* (Little, Brown, 1964); for disarmament, Richard J. Barnet, *Who Wants Disarmament?*

(Boston, 1960), Arthur I. Waskow, *The Limits of Defense* (Garden City, 1962), Amitai Etzioni, *The Hard Way to Peace* (New York, 1962), J. David Singer, *Deterrence, Arms Control, and Disarmament* (Columbus, 1962); and Walter Millis, *An End to Arms* (New York, 1965).

Important efforts to examine the mathematical theory of games as it might be applied to military strategy, and to begin developing a general theory of conflict, have been made by Thomas C. Schelling in *The Strategy of Conflict* (Cambridge, 1960); by Kenneth Boulding in *Conflict and Defense* (New York, 1962), and by Anatol Rapoport in *Fights, Games, and Debates* (Ann Arbor, 1960). Rapoport later criticized the whole strategic mode of thought as applied to international conflict, in a study called *Strategy and Conscience* (New York, 1964).

There has been no satisfactory full-length examination of the impact of the Cold War and military strategy upon American domestic politics and society. The various attempts have included C. Wright Mills, *The Power Elite* (New York, 1956) and *The Causes of World War Three* (New York, 1958), Jack Raymond, *Power in the Pentagon* (New York, 1964), John M. Swomley, *The Military Establishment* (Boston, 1964), Harry Howe Ransom, *Can American Democracy Survive Cold War?* (New York, 1964), and Fred J. Cook, *The Warfare State* (New York, 1962). One of the few efforts to examine the implications of world disarmament for American domestic life is by Louis Henkin, *Arms Control and Inspection in American Law* (New York, 1958).

The economic impacts of defense and disarmament have been more adequately studied. See especially Charles J. Hitch and Roland N. McKean, *The Economics of Defense in the Nuclear Age* (Cambridge, 1960) and Emile Benoit and Kenneth Boulding, eds., *Disarmament and the Economy* (New York, 1963).

Ethical and religious problems raised by the advent of thermonuclear weapons have been only tentatively explored in most American writing, but see Thomas Merton, ed., *Breakthrough to Peace* (New York, 1962), Paul Ramsey, *War and the Christian Conscience* (Durham, 1961), Robert W. Tucker, *The Just War* (Baltimore, 1960), and John C. Bennett, ed., *Nuclear Weapons and the Conflict of Conscience* (New York, 1962).

Among the few works explicitly discussing military strategy in the context of world political configurations have been Robert Osgood, *NATO: The Entangling Alliance* (Quadrangle, 1962), Alastair Buchan, *NATO in the Sixties* (Harper, 1963), and Marcus Raskin and Richard Barnet, *After Twenty Years* (New York, 1965).

Since Sputnik, there have been published four important successive collections of papers, each emerging from the joint work of a conference of scholars on aspects of military strategy, arms control, and international conflict. These are Donald G. Brennan, ed., *Arms Control, Disarmament, and National Security* (New York, 1961); Seymour Melman, ed., *Disarmament: Its Politics and Economics* (Boston, 1962); Roger Fisher, ed., *International Conflict and Behavioral Science: The Craigville Papers* (New York, 1964); and Richard A. Falk and Richard J. Barnet, eds., *Security in Disarmament* (Princeton, 1965).

During the period covered by this volume, the American journals most frequently examining problems of military strategy and international conflict at the level of well-informed public debate were *Bulletin of the Atomic Scientists, Foreign Affairs, Liberation,* and *War/Peace Report*. More scholarly material could be found in *World Politics, Journal of Conflict Resolution, Journal of Arms Control,* and *Disarmament and Arms Control*. Any study of the sources should include material published in military or military-industrial journals like *Aviation Week, General Electric Defense Quarterly, Army,* and *U. S. Naval Institute Proceedings;* the hearings held and published each year on the military budget by the House and Senate Subcommittees on Military Appropriations; and the *Hearings on Military Posture* published each year by the House Committee on Armed Services.